AMSTERDAM... THE ESSENCE

A view of a great European city, in the words
of the people who shape it.

DAVID BECKETT

Portrait photography **Joost van Manen** | *City photography* **Pim Kops** | *Art Direction & Design* **Sarah Loughran**

WWW.THEESSENCEONLINE.COM

AMSTERDAM... THE ESSENCE

Published by DJB Pubs BV, Netherlands, 2011

Copyright 2011 © David Beckett

Printed in the Netherlands by Pantheon Drukkers, Velsen Noord. *www.pantheondrukkers.nl*

ISBN – 978-94-90874-02-5

ACKNOWLEDGEMENTS

Working together is in the DNA of Amsterdam, and this book is a physical proof of the supportive and creative powers that exist all around this great city. The people who helped make the book are the true essence of Amsterdam.

Special thanks go to Joost van Manen, for helping me so much by adding his outstanding Professional Photography skills to the portrait images.

www.joostvanmanen.com

Special thanks in equal measure to Pim Kops for sharing his amazing city photographs. It's been a genuine honour to learn about his "way of looking" at Amsterdam.

www.facebook.com/pimkopspage

Sarah Loughran, for bringing the book to life with amazing design.

www.spheredesign.biz

Anique van der Hulst, for ideas generation and publicity genius.

www.nineteen.eu

All the interviewees, for their time and spirit of openness to something new.

Sheila Schenkel, for intensive final editing, long scooter rides, advice and support; and for being the best sounding board and friend possible during the development of The Essence™. (*Zeger is proud of you, out in the blue.*)

Matthew Curlewis, for excellent *Stretch and Tone* writers' classes, and enabling great feedback from the group.

Philo van Kamenade, for creating excellent mini-documentaries.

Marinca Kaldeway, for a great translation of Youp's *Het Laatste Woord*.

Laser 3.14, for sharing his vision of Amsterdam and being a constant support.

Mark de Kruijk and the Westergasfabriek, for supporting the launch event.

Pascal Griffioen, for being so co-operative and supportive even before the project took shape, as well as for his great Essence painting [p. 56].

Youp van 't Hek, for providing an excellent *Het Laatste Woord*

Geerte Udo and Bapke Wiebols at *I amsterdam*, for sharing values of celebrating our city's qualities.

Bob de Boers, for a constant stream of suggestions and for putting me in contact with many of the interviewees.

René at Pantheon Drukkers, for being more than 'just a printer' and giving craftsman-like service.

Brant Emery and Sandra Karis for 'The Kitchen of Ideas.'©

David Freed, for great editing.

Renata Harper, for excellent proofreading.

Ian de Jong, for interview transcriptions.

Wouter Boes, for filming Youp.

Siobhan Reynolds, for constant friendship and last-minute proofreading.

Morten Brix, for continual support and advice as a business colleague and friend over many years; and Christine Brix-Ho, for years of hospitality and friendship.

Sonny and Peter Stroex-Carr, for listening and friendship since 1998.

Nicki Davies, for helping me develop the kernel of this idea in the streets of Buenos Aires and on the hills of New Zealand.

Kathleen Warners, for listening to my essence tales over white wine and dinner in the huiskamerrestaurant.

Sally Roddy, for *Tango – The Truth*, a book that was the first seed of inspiration for The Essence™.

Silvia Herrera, for believing in me.

Xavier Baars, for recommending *Rework*. Reading that book made me decide to get on with it.

Jan De Block, for "You are a creator now!"

Lance Miller, for teaching me that 'Presentation is 9 points of the law'.

Canon, for many years of great working life.

Toru Sato, for suggesting I should come to Amsterdam in the first place and helping me stay when it got tough in the first months.

Jo Parfitt, for high quality publishing consultancy and workshops.

Mike Beckett, for being the best role model a father could be; for helping me to see that 'every company needs more than one product'; and for constant advice and support during this project and throughout the rest of my life.

Kay Beckett, for passing on to me the quality of getting up no matter what knocks you down.

Peter Beckett, for being a great man and brother.

Tom Robinson, for musical and lyrical inspiration since 1978 and for suggesting *The Artists' Way* by Julia Cameron. Without that, I would never have believed all of this could be possible. (Oh, and thanks also for *The One*.)

Marillion, for the line, 'Choose life, choose living, go digging for essence'.

Rogier & Carmen van Duivenbooden, Margot Koeleman, Eveline van Moppes, Amal Chatterjee, Tim Butler, Zora Minarikova, Karin Smets, Bruce Haase, Eelco Meesters, Andrea Arlow, Sarah Casey, Mieke Tummers, Chantal and Frank Timmer, Yvonne Bardzinska and the Angel Mafia, The Li clan, Delphine Bedel, Rick Lightstone, Luke Nyman, Laura Watkinson, Hania Sobolewska; for various help, advice, inspiration, support and friendship along the way.

First 25 fans on Facebook

Thanks for your faith before anything even existed of The Essence™!

Karin Smets, Anna Farrell, Nicolas Nguyen, Carmen Maqueda van Duivenbooden, Gerald Schneider, Omer Zimmer, Martina Miholic, Vitor Spencer, Matti Hämäläinen, Kristina Vitkevicute, Angeline Wennekes, Bruce Haase, Monica Prah, Carole Greenland, Morten Brix, Manuela Diwisch, Jure Culiberg, Caterina Bonfiglio, Ewa Martynek, Floris Blok, Jill Li, Margot Koeleman, Marta Garcia Rodriguez, Agnieszka Mruk, Romana Maitz-Pollak.

And finally, thanks to Eric Cantona for *the* guiding advice of the whole project.

"You have to trust your team-mates, always. If not, we are lost."*

I followed this idea whenever I didn't know what to do during the development of this book. Somehow, one of my many team-mates mentioned above came up with ideas and solutions for every situation.

It's no longer my book; it became *our* book.

From the movie, 'Looking for Eric', Dir Ken Loach

CONTENTS

INTRODUCTION

Amsterdam is perhaps the most enigmatic city in the world: you can live here for years and still not know what truly makes things happen.

It's a small place with an enormous reputation. Mention to anyone around the globe that you live in Amsterdam, and the reaction is universal: "How cool, that must be a great place to live!" Yet despite being recognised as one of the world's great cities, the Netherlands' capital is not like London or Paris. There's no Big Ben or Eiffel Tower here. When Amsterdam's five million yearly visitors are asked why they come, they answer, "For the atmosphere." Yes, most visit the fabulous Van Gogh Museum and take a boat ride along the canals – but their main interest is to take in the special surroundings and the 'feel' of the city.

In the '60s, Amsterdam was named 'The Magic Centre'. For me, that sums up the special quality of this city that enthralls visitors and expatriates from around the world.

I first moved to Amsterdam to work for Canon in 1998 and quickly fell in love with living here. When my job was moved to England in 2009, without hesitation I resolved to remain in my favourite city - and not long after, decided to write a book about what I now consider to be my home-town. Yet, despite my long association with Amsterdam, I couldn't honestly say I understood its true essence. As I was pondering this, a chance occurrence led me in the direction of telling the city's story in the words of the people who shape it. Coming across a Texan musician as she played acoustic guitar out of a first-floor Prinsengracht window on Queen's Day set me on a path of discovery that I could never have planned. Then again, in the words of Paul Spies [p. 36], "Nothing in Amsterdam is planned – everything is an outcome!"

The development of this book matches one aspect of the true spirit of the city. I began with nothing more than an idea and a lot of enthusiasm for a rough concept called The Essence, and that concept took firm shape through fantastic co-operation from a diverse group of Amsterdammers. Every time I contacted possible interviewees, they showed the straightforward attitude of appreciating a creative project.: *He's trying to do something new, let's be part of it.* It is exactly this spirit that has helped me bring *Amsterdam... The Essence* come to life.

What followed was a year-long experience of encounters with fascinating characters while discovering new music venues, art galleries and entrepreneur meet-up groups. I came face to face with an anonymous street artist, protested against anti-gay violence, sat in a Red Light District window for an evening, and conducted two interviews in the Dutch houses of parliament. No matter how famous or successful, everyone involved generously offered their time and wished me the best of luck. Each time I met with these people, they taught me something new about our city.

There are countless travel guides about Amsterdam, and they do a great job of telling you where to go and what to do. *Amsterdam... The Essence* brings you closer to answering the most intriguing question of all: why is the city like it is?

Enjoy discovering the essence of Amsterdam.

A new city appears in winter. A place that can be cold, yet also cosy and welcoming. It was snowing when Lake Montgomery first came to Amsterdam and still she fell in love with its charm.

PAULUS POTTERSTRAAT

THE ATMOSPHERE OF FREEDOM IN AMSTERDAM MADE ME BOLD AS A PERFORMER

LAKE MONTGOMERY

AMSTERDAMMER SINCE 2002
SINGER/SONGWRITER
FAVOURITE AMSTERDAM LOCATION – WG-PLEIN

As I ambled along the canals on 30 April 2010, my mind was partly on the development of this book, and partly on the fact that my Heineken was getting warm and needed replacing.

That date is Queen's Day, a yearly celebration of the monarch's birthday. It starts with a huge open market involving everyone emptying their cupboards and cellars, piling everything they can find onto the pavements and selling it for whatever they can get. A distinctive aspect of the experience is also the music. As the day progresses, revellers set up speakers outside their windows, play drums in the street and load disco gear onto boats. Seeing a cool, tiny woman in her mid-20s playing acoustic guitar in a window on Prinsengracht caught my attention that day. I listened for a few minutes and was especially taken with the song 'Amsterdam'. A friend of hers enthusiastically waved a CD for sale under my nose, bearing the singer's name.

Who wouldn't be intrigued by a musician called Lake Montgomery?

A day later, CD in hand, I checked her Myspace site and it became clear that Lake's Amsterdam story is very different to mine. Maybe she could tell me something new about this city? Perhaps she might have an insight into the real essence of Amsterdam.

This sparked an idea and I wrote an email requesting an interview. While waiting for her reply, I began to realise this might just be the approach for my book that I'd been looking for: talking to people who represent the crossroads of diversity that is Amsterdam, in order to tell the story of the city from as many different points of view as possible.

Lake replied a few days later and we met at WG Café on a sunny, Amsterdam spring day.

And so the journey began.

"I was living happily in New Orleans, but when the flood happened, it broke my heart. I got the chance to go to Orléans in France – Old Orleans – when the city offered a gift to 20 students to come to France and study – free tickets, free apartment. I took up the chance and this brought me to Europe.

Lake first came to Amsterdam in a similar way to many others I've met – randomly, but destined to end up here.

My first visit to Amsterdam was in 2002 to see a friend and, while in Orléans, I came back many times. The intention was to stay in Amsterdam for a month only, because my ticket back to New Orleans was due to expire. It turned out differently after I met an artist through some modelling work, and he asked me to stay for a year as his model.

He lived in a small town in the very north of the Netherlands called Uithuizen, and that's where I learned Dutch. Many of the villagers had been Amsterdammers in the '60s, but had moved to cheaper houses in the countryside during the '70s and '80s.

I used to come to Amsterdam with my guitar and for the first time I felt like playing in public. That was a barrier back home, but there was something about Amsterdam that helped me become bold as a performer.

Many musicians develop their skills through school or being pushed by parents. In Lake's case, her pets were her first audience.

The first time I picked up the guitar was at the age of 16. It was odd because I was more focused on writing poetry at the time and believed I was going to be a writer. To begin with, I just played for myself and my cats, and that progressed to taking my guitar along to parties. I'd play a couple of tunes and received some positive responses, but I kept it very small.

In America there's something that really blocks me from performing. If you want to play, it means you must *want* to be a superstar; you're supposed to want to be a rockstar. That really kept me from trying to pursue getting gigs and a career as a musician.

What was different when I came to Amsterdam? I just felt more confident. I was a bit exotic being a black American, bluesy performer, and it felt like this was the right place for me. The freedom, the diversity, being able to speak English yet not live in America – these afforded some kind of comfort. I was really inspired to play and that's when I started performing, just busking on the streets.

Things fell into place in Amsterdam. There are so many venues to play at here, where it doesn't matter if nobody knows you. They just want to hear some music.

People from outside think Amsterdam is a huge city – they're often surprised to hear it has only three quarters of a million inhabitants. That smaller, manageable size meant I fell into the music scene pretty quickly. Rapid-fire connections happen all the time and that makes the music scene here very accessible for a newcomer.

The Amsterdam Songwriters Guild [ASG] helps a lot. It's a group of talented musicians who support each other, do gigs together, make bookings for each other – man, that's one big reason why I live here!

One example: last year I did a street music tour with a couple of ASG musicians and we played 26 streets in the city in three days – we called it 'Amsterdam A-Z' and got a lot of newspaper coverage. That's the kind of stuff that still goes on here. It makes me proud. I don't know where else I could be doing my musical thing.

It's certainly a typical spring day for this city – half an hour after we start, the clouds come over and cold rain sends us scurrying inside the café. As we warm up, she explains how she's reached a good level of Dutch in just a few years.

It's difficult to improve your Dutch speaking skills here because of the high level of English that almost everyone seems to have. For me, language is all about touching a native feeling; it's a must if you really want to get into the people and the society. I don't think I would feel so 'inside' without speaking Dutch.

We all want clarity in communication and you're offered this bridge of perfect English, but then you swim and scramble around in the cold waters of Dutch language while you're learning and it can be really hard. But if you manage to speak your way through that, there is a secret world of local culture that opens up to you.

Nevertheless, my songs are in English and I tell stories in them. It's a big advantage that, although I'm in a foreign country, the audience can understand these stories.

When I ask Lake about her favourite venues to perform at, I realise that, even after many years of living here, there's still so much to learn. I have never been to most of the places she mentions.

It's great to play at the Dwazezaken, a café with beautiful, high, red mosaic ceilings and an excellent sound system. OCCII on Amstelveenseweg is fun too – it used to be a squat but it's a cultural centre now. OT301 is another former squat with lots of creative happenings and there's a fantastic organic/vegetarian restaurant inside. You need to reserve, and they serve you a two-course meal priced at a 'donation' of between 5–10 euros, depending on your income. That's the kind of stuff I like, you know, the surprises that you won't see in the guidebooks.

Also 't Blijvertje is a really sweet place to play. It's another squat but not a legalised one, so you don't know when it might just disappear.

My link to Amsterdam has been all about music. Most of my network here is built from those who have seen me perform, and I sing wherever I possibly can to get to know more people. When I'm onstage, I'm just being myself and the audience feel they learn about me through the music – sometimes when I come off, I get hugs from strangers! But they feel they already know something about me because of the songs and lyrics. I'm just trusting in my craft to open everything up for me, and it's worked so far.

Amsterdam seems to have touched a nerve and sparked Lake's creativity. There's something truly inspiring about her story – coming out here, a long way from home, and getting started by playing on the streets. And her jail story is also impressive!

While I was living in Orléans, I think I developed a little crush on Amsterdam through visiting so often. I was still an outsider in Europe and visiting was like therapy. I do feel like a foreigner here, but comfortably so. I like the curiosity that being a foreigner provokes in others – there's not much of a negative side to it here. Maybe that's part of who I am; I like to be different.

Amsterdam becomes really sweet in winter, even though it gets so dark in the long nights. I was captured by how beautiful it is and that whole combination inspired me to play music on the streets. This was a great step because I got to see how the people were living their lives; I had a lot of chance conversations with locals who responded to the music. It was a kind of training, getting pieces of life from passers-by and developing the music through their appreciation, rather than trying to making a living immediately.

This all led me to write a song called 'Amsterdam' about my first experiences here – it was a love song to my crush-city. But I've also had a less positive experience of being a foreigner in Europe. 'Like a Timebomb' is a number that's all about being put in jail because I didn't have my passport on me…

THERE ARE SO MANY DIFFERENT PEOPLE COMING TO AMSTERDAM FOR SO MANY DIFFERENT REASONS. EVERYBODY'S GOT A NEW, INTERESTING STORY

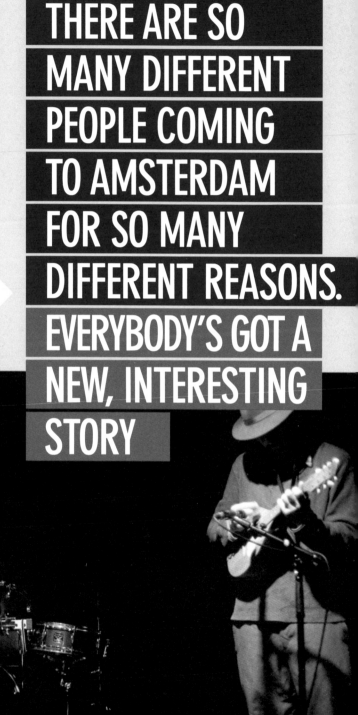

I was coming into France from Spain and the customs officials thought I was African. I didn't realise I had lost my American passport until I got to the border. As a result I was first put in jail for two days, then transported to an immigrant retention centre with a lot of Africans and Mexicans. It was prison – they kept saying it wasn't, but there were iron bars over the windows and cops with guns; I couldn't even touch my guitar in case I used it as a deadly weapon! They kept me there for a week until the case was heard.

It was kind of funny when the translator in the courtroom said to me, "You're Nigerian, right?" No – try again. "Senegalese?" Nope. When I told him I was from Texas, no one believed it! As soon as it was established that I was a fine upstanding American, they just let me go.

That night, I had nowhere to go and so I asked to stay an extra 12 hours in jail. They treated me so differently as soon as they realised I was American. I got my guitar back, it was all handshakes and joking around – just because the judge's signature said I was okay.

The CD I bought on Queen's Day is *Lake Montgomery: Live in Amsterdam*. She explains how Dutch film director Suzanne Raes *[see her interview on page 122]* helped her to stage a live concert in a canal house.

I met Suzanne through an artists' project that she managed and we stayed in contact. I talked with her about how much I wanted to make a CD but how I just didn't enjoy playing in a recording studio. That's something I definitely have to – and will – develop, but at that stage I felt at my best when performing live.

Suzanne said, "No problem – we can do a concert in my front room." I could hardly believe it, but that is typical of her and, I guess, typical of this city. There have been so many people who have given all kinds of support to help me survive here.

We cleared her living room, created a little stage, and she arranged for a sound engineer to capture everything. I felt great with an audience of around 30 friends and we made the CD on a very low budget. I can hardly thank Suzanne enough.

Lake is one of many, on some kind of a journey, who pass through Amsterdam and find it holds them for a period. Something tells me she might just be somewhere else this time next year.

Serendipity guides my life. I'm not big on plans; I just end up where I end up. The need to keep moving feels almost genetic and being 'the traveller' is part of me, so leaving is maybe inevitable at some stage. I do get that itch, but there's something about Amsterdam that suits my character as it is right now. It's hard to imagine another

OUTSIDERS THINK AMSTERDAM IS A HUGE CITY. THEY'RE ALWAYS SURPRISED TO HEAR IT'S ONLY THREE QUARTERS OF A MILLION PEOPLE

city where I could have started playing music as a professional so comfortably – and once you get a good start, you don't want to face starting all over again. It takes time to be trusted, and I've managed to build up a good fan base here, with some shows planned over the next few months. I always say I'm gonna stay here till my last gig.

A friend described me as the kind of person who would just leave one day, maybe not even saying goodbye, and call later to say that I'd moved to Bangladesh or South America. I do understand that if you keep moving, people are not so willing to trust you. I like what I've started here and I'll stay to make the connections stronger and enjoy the feeling I have about the city.

www.lakemontgomery.com,
www.myspace.com/lakemontgomery

WILHELMINA STATUE ON THE ROKIN

The Dutch attitude to monarchy is a little different to that of most countries. Simple tributes like this figure of former Queen Wilhelmina are in keeping with how Amsterdam views its royals. Henk Schiffmacher also has some interesting opinions on this – and many other – subjects.

I FELL IN LOVE WITH THE AMSTERDAM ABILITY TO COMMUNICATE

HENK SCHIFFMACHER - AKA HANKY PANKY

AMSTERDAMMER SINCE 1972
TATTOO ARTIST AND WRITER
FAVOURITE AMSTERDAM LOCATION – AMSTELDIJK, ALONG THE AMSTEL RIVER

"If you write a book about Amsterdam, you have to include Hanky Panky."

Who?

I checked out my friend's recommendation and found this to be the nickname of Henk Schiffmacher – a true Amsterdam character and tattooist to the stars.

The Red Hot Chili Peppers, Kurt Cobain, Dutch artist and singer Herman Brood and Robbie Williams are amongst his many famous clients. When I called his shop to make an appointment, they misheard my name and said, "David Beckham?" It was as almost if they were expecting him.

Henk is a burly guy who looks like a cross between a Hell's Angel and a yeti. And man, can he talk!

Golden teeth glinting, he boomed out his opinions and stories in the middle of his tattoo parlour at Ceintuurbaan 416, surrounded by his work and a bunch of buzzing young artists hanging on his every word.

I'd expected to be led to an office, but Henk is informal, to say the least. A poster showing his involvement in an Aids Foundation campaign points to his fame in the Netherlands – he was one of four faces featured to promote the cause. Yet the poster adorns the toilet door, a sign of the straightforward Amsterdammer that he is.

We sit and talk (well, he talks...) and I have to admit to being a little in awe of all the framed records and mementos on the wall from singer

Anouk, the Chilis, Van Halen and many others.

He also surrounds himself with numerous books about his art – including a few he's written himself. Henk might appear a little rough, but appearances should certainly not deceive. He's a highly knowledgeable man with heartfelt views on Amsterdam and tattooing.

This city is incredible; we live in an open-air museum. They should just take all the cars out of the city and make it accessible for pedestrians. It's the shop owners who prevented that, but I think they're wrong. As soon as you empty the streets of cars, you can use the canal to get everyone in and out of the city.

Henk launches into his story before I've even asked a question. He's a man of many opinions and always fascinating to listen to, especially when he reminisces about his early days in the Dutch capital.

I had a very bad start at school. They didn't recognise dyslexia in those days, and my father helped me learn with a piece of wood. Write it down – wrong – *boom!* Then he would hit me again until I learned it. I had to get a job as young as possible, just to get away.

When I was 14, I was working in a sandwich shop in my hometown of Harderwijk, often till one or two in the morning. The guys I worked with would take me to Amsterdam in an old Pontiac Firebird and get me drunk, and then shove me into the whorehouses. I was having a hell of a time!

They used to take me to this one café called Jan Heuvel. It had a round table that was always full of characters from all kinds of backgrounds – art dealers, pimps, tax-men, musicians. They were storytellers and they knew how to tell it right. They wouldn't hesitate to stand on the table or stick their head in a sink of water, just to make sure their story was good. I was fascinated with all that; I fell in love with the Amsterdam ability to communicate. Where I came from, it was not at all done to stand up and make yourself noticed. I felt I'd found my home, a place where my character belonged.

Of course, booze was a big part of those early experiences. In my village, alcohol was very hidden – liquor stores had blinds in front of the window and you came out with an anonymous brown bag. As for sex, well, it didn't exist in my time! The '60s changed a lot here, thank God...

As he talks, a cool Japanese guy with samurai-style ponytail and a body covered in colourful tattoos is advising a young customer. "This is the art I can do for you," he says.

The city's creative spirit clearly drew out a side of Henk's character when he arrived.

When you're young, Amsterdam completely shapes you. I wanted to be a fucking artistic person, that's why I came to the city. For me, it was a development, an escape from Harderwijk, and I worked on anything that was even a little bit creative – window design, sign painting, anything I could find.

Later I worked at department store, de Bijenkorf, where I learned my photography and graphic design skills. I was doing fashion shoots with a studio full of beautiful Dutch models – that was a great job!

I had to go to Ibiza with seven or eight of them – tough, huh? They even took me to Japan as their toy boy.

I came back and picked up my tattooing hobby. I was able to use a basement owned by the former president of the Hells Angels, Willem. Once, 12,000 G.I.s came to Amsterdam and I can tell you, I did a lot of tattoos that weekend. It made me think I should go ahead and make a real business out of it. I did pretty much everything in life like this, with no real plan – things just sort of happened.

Luck played its part. Firstly, I set up in a world-famous city, and my old shop was in the Red Light District. No matter who you are, every visitor ends up having a look there, doing a little 'window-shopping'. My big break came when I tattooed the Red Hot Chili Peppers. If it had been any other band, no matter how big, the tattoos wouldn't have been on display, but the Chilis used the tattoos as part of their image building – and it helped that they were doing every video butt-naked! Mine were the rock and roll tattoos with the most TV coverage ever.

The Chilis would tell their friends, "You gotta go see Henk in Amsterdam", and that's what they did. The shop looked like the dressing room of the Paradiso, one of Amsterdam's most famous music venues; and to be honest, I didn't know half of them – I had no idea who the fuck Kurt Cobain was when he came in.

Once Henk had established himself, he wanted to share some of his knowledge and passion for his profession. This extended to writing books and founding his wonderful museum.

When I started out as a photographer, taking pictures of people who are tattooed, I wanted to make a book immediately. But I realised I shouldn't be too quick. *Make a decent book,* I thought, *'Never hurt what you love' – don't be in too much of a hurry.* So I started to look more deeply into the why, where and how of tattooing as an art. There is no end to this thing and I've chronicled that development in my books.

Searching around the history of tattooing is like discovering the world – it's related to the migration of tribes, to religion, has a social aspect, a criminology aspect... It's a very exciting art form to be involved in. I'm trying to educate others about this stuff; that's why I've written histories and a book called *The Encyclopedia for the Art and History of Tattooing.*

I got the keys to the building of my new museum today. I had a small one before, but at a certain point I decided to split the collection. I was thinking about sharing it with different museums, but all of them came back to me and said, "Hold on to the character of this collection, keep it together."

The new museum will be in a great area, in the east of the city. There you have the Hermitage, the Jewish History Museum, then the Hortus Botanicus, the Hollandsche Schouwburg, Resistance Museum, Artis, the Zoological Museum, and our tattoo museum next to the Tropen. I'm gonna fight to get the Museum Quarter relocated!

I had somehow expected Henk to be a man of strong political views

THE SHOP LOOKED LIKED THE DRESSING ROOM OF THE PARADISO. I DIDN'T KNOW HALF OF THEM - I HAD NO IDEA WHO THE F**K KURT COBAIN WAS WHEN HE CAME IN

and maybe once that was the case. He is openly disappointed with some of the city's changes in the past years, but still has a balanced view of the consequences of change for Amsterdam.

I lost my trust in politicians during the Nieuwmarkt riots in the '70s – you know, when all the squatters were thrown out of their buildings so the metro could be built. We were hippies in those days and we thought we were going to change the world, but it didn't happen. I never had much trust in the law and politics – we should have kept it to the Ten Commandments and left it at that.

Our city's beautiful and special, but a lot of the renovation planning is made from a table in an office and not from the street. That planning should be done closer to the people, because Amsterdam *is* the people. Right at the beginning, I was against the new metro line they're building through the centre of the city, but I hope they finish it now. If you want to manage a city, you have to look way ahead – so sometimes you have to do stuff that's not really popular at that moment, and stick to the vision you have.

I ask Henk about the background to the Aids foundation poster on the bathroom door.

I donated a bunch of money to the Aids foundation, and had good contact with them. I also worked as an ambassador for an organisation called Orange Babies, helping raise money to build

WHEN I TATTOOED THE RED HOT CHILI PEPPERS, THEY WERE DOING EVERY VIDEO BUTT-NAKED

hospitals in Africa and support HIV-affected mothers there. If your face gets a bit known, you get asked to be involved in different charities. I've been a bad boy in many situations during my life so I think to myself, *Why not be the nice guy for a while?* Best to polish up my karma a little bit – and you never know, the Queen might still give me a fucking medal!

Nowadays I go to these functions and the Queen sits on one side, Prince Willem-Alexander on the other. Think of it – I'm there next to the goddamn Queen, arms covered in tattoos. That was impossible 30 years ago. We took this art somewhere, you know; it's not only for criminals, prostitutes and sailors – although I love tattooing criminals, prostitutes and sailors! They're some of the best customers.

By the end of our talk, my overwhelming impression of Henk is of a bold and creative man who goes around inspiring and challenging, no matter what situation he finds himself in. I imagine, though, that in royal company he might tone himself down a little.

Am I quiet with the Queen? Sorry, I really don't know any other way to be! I'm just me, like me or hate me. As far as I'm concerned, the Queen has the same value as my mother has or any other woman for that matter. I called her ma'am, and I was told I shouldn't have. Well, sorry, but 'Your Majesty' is not in my vocabulary!

www.henkschiffmacher.nl

THAT COMBINATION OF FEELING LIKE YOU'RE IN A VILLAGE YET BEING IN A WORLD-RENOWNED CITY IS UNIQUE

HALINA REIJN

AMSTERDAMMER SINCE 1992
STAR OF OVER 30 PLAYS AND 15 FILMS
FAVOURITE AMSTERDAM LOCATION – LEIDSEPLEIN

One evening in early 2009, my plans to go to the glorious old Tuschinski cinema, near Rembrandtplein, were thwarted. As I approached the nearby Muntplein, I saw that the streets were cordoned off.

The next day, I learned that Hollywood movie *Valkyrie* had premiered there; its star, Tom Cruise, appeared with Amsterdam co-stars Halina Reijn and Carice van Houten. As I read the newspaper, and looked at the pictures of the event, it all seemed so incredibly glamorous and far away from my life.

Fast-forward 20 months and I find myself sitting with Halina at the EYE Film Institute, in the centre of Vondelpark. The magic of introducing a renowned star into this book is highlighted for me when we walk through the front doors together: an elderly lady gazes at her and speaks her name with genuine wonder, giving the word 'Halina' a special aura.

However, as is typical of Amsterdam, Halina turns out to be straightforward and unaffected by the adoration and red carpet treatment.

We meet on a cold, snowbound day. I'd expected her to arrive by taxi, but instead she makes her way across the icy city by bike – just as 60 percent of the population travels in Amsterdam. I'd arranged the shoot with a professional photographer and friend of mine, Joost van Manen, and we'd wondered if she would also prefer to have a make-up artist on hand. To our surprise, Halina is quite happy to be captured with her natural looks. All very impressive.

Halina is a true communicator, performing on stage and in film, as well as being regularly seen on a popular primetime Dutch TV show. She has also written a novel called *Prinsesje Nooitgenoeg* and is now working on a new film script. Before telling her story of coming from the northern city of Groningen to the capital, she gives a glimpse into the world of the Amsterdam paparazzi.

"That's the great thing about Amsterdam. It's like New York – even if you've been on TV or in movies, you can just walk around, ignored, like anyone else. I love that element of the Dutch mentality; we don't treat others with *too* much reverence.

While I was promoting *Valkyrie* with Tom Cruise, I saw what happens to him in places like London – people screaming and crowding around him all the time. Carice [van Houten] and I loved being part of that for a while – we were like little kids, because it was a novelty for us – but it got to be too much very quickly. Our car was constantly chased, and if we took one step out of our hotel we were almost raped by the photographers! I would never want to live that life permanently. Amsterdam is so much easier.

You do see paparazzi here sometimes, but you have to laugh because it's on a really small scale. On one occasion, a friend and I were being bothered while having lunch in Amsterdam Zuid [South], so we rode off on our bikes and they chased after us. When we reached the border of that area, they stopped! Why didn't they follow us to our house? Because they think to themselves, "This is our neighbourhood, and we can't be bothered to go any further."

We're sitting at the spacious mezzanine of the EYE and Halina's voice rings through the building, her animated limbs accentuating her words. This continual movement from an accomplished actress shouldn't surprise me, but her refreshing openness certainly does. It's great to hear her very 'normal' stories of being afraid of the big city when first arriving.

I was born in Amsterdam, but moved just a couple of months later. My parents were living in a tiny apartment and they decided to move out – a typical Amsterdam story of the '70s, having too little space costing too much money. Also they had that kind of hippie wish to raise their kids closer to nature, so we moved to Groningen.

When I started in youth theatre at 17, some casting directors noticed me, and before I knew it, I was whisked off to Amsterdam for auditions. I got a role in a TV show and the production company put me in this beautiful apartment near Sarphatipark – but I was so alone and frightened of the city! I felt it was my enemy. You know my biggest fear? Cycling. I'd been told, "Look out for the tram lines. Don't get your wheel stuck in them." Well I'm pretty clumsy, so I was all over the place and constantly trapping myself in those tram tracks.

Then my second biggest fear came true – mice! It was the first time I had lived away from home, so I didn't really clean anything properly. Suddenly there were mice all over the apartment, and I was so ashamed that I didn't tell anyone about it.

The city was such a contrast to the smaller world of Groningen, especially as I had been studying at a Steiner school – very protected

and new age – so the real world had just passed me by. Suddenly I found myself in this world of TV celebrities, being dragged to a lot of celebrity parties where I didn't know anybody. If there was no party, I just sat at home, reading.

When I did go out, I kept losing my way. Well, I'm very bad at directions anyway; even now I can get disoriented in Amsterdam, but at that time I was almost permanently lost!

It's funny to look back on that period, because now I see the city just as a large village. Back then it was so scary for me that after two years I decided to go to theatre school in Maastricht, just to avoid staying here. There were offers to work in Amsterdam, so I could have chosen not to go to theatre school and immediately focus on movies and TV, but I didn't feel at home here.

In a way, Halina's initial fear of Amsterdam led her to develop further her theatrical talents. It's a surprise to hear of her discomfort because onstage she seems so much in control.

Certainly, as I became better known, I noticed that some have this idea that I'm very powerful and "raarrggh!" *[Halina growls a kind of big-cat roar, her arms splayed wide in mock, fearless attack.]* They're surprised when I tell them I am frightened about something simple.

Acting in movies and TV is a tough way to start your career, so I'm very grateful my worries about Amsterdam pushed me to theatre school. When I did finally come back here, it was easier because my boyfriend moved here too, meaning we had a kind of security in each other. I was still frightened, but I gave it a shot. After three weeks of playing the role of Ophelia in a production of *Hamlet*, I seemed to wake up suddenly and started to love it here. I began to discover the city, because finally I had colleagues and friends, which of course makes a big difference.

Over the years, I've met some people who come to Amsterdam and leave after a short period, seeming not to 'get' the city. You have to search under the surface of this town; otherwise you miss it. Halina found it easier in America.

I lived in LA for a year. Many think it's a horrible city, but I loved it because the people are very welcoming to a stranger. Okay, you can see it as fake, but they did what nobody in Holland will do. You never invite a stranger to your house here, and my LA friends find that really weird. You have to make friends before you can enjoy being in Amsterdam. Maybe most cities are like that, but Americans are more open and easily invite you into their lives – "Come over and I'll show you around" – whereas we stick to our own circle of friends here.

Language is an issue and if you want to get to know real Amsterdammers, learning Dutch will speed things up. Then again, more than 40 percent of those living in this city are not Dutch. Recently our theatre company started performances with English surtitles [like subtitles, but above the stage] twice a week. Yesterday it was great – the audience was much more international.

Amsterdam has a lot of contradictions. On the one hand you live in a supposedly major world city, with a big image and inhabitants of

all kinds of nationalities; and on the other hand, it's a tiny place. You can ride around on your bicycle between small neighbourhoods, and get anywhere in 10 minutes. I like that unique contrast. I travel a lot with my work, but I've never seen this combination of being in a village – like, really in a village, where you can meet your friends by accident – and yet having all the shops and everything you want. Amsterdam has the benefits of a big city, but stays small.

If I'm in New York for a while, I miss those qualities. Amsterdam is not so flashy or glamorous and most of the time I love that about this city, but after a while I get *sick* of it! You feel like the whole place is on your head, and then you really have to get away.

The press-officer of the Film Institute brings us coffee and Halina is polite and sincere in her thanks. The Amsterdam attitude is captured in the phrase *'Doe maar gewoon, dan doe je al gek genoeg'* ['Just be normal, that's weird enough'], and that keeps everyone grounded – even Hollywood stars. Still, Halina has some frustrations with the concept from a creative point of view.

All that *'doe maar gewoon'* stuff – it can feel like 'Don't be unusual or out of the ordinary'. In other countries, they are much more open to admiring something extraordinary, whereas here, it's a case of playing everything down. That does have a positive influence as well; you could say there is a built-in barrier to acceptance here that forces you to think about everything you're doing and ensures good quality.

Nevertheless, I found it was great to be in the USA for a while, just so I could re-invent myself. A scholarship was offered to me for acting lessons in another country, and a movie I appeared in had an Oscar nomination, so it made sense for me to take the classes in LA. I had a lot of meetings with directors for a couple of weeks, and very quickly became really depressed, because I had to humiliate myself and start all over again; I had no existing network. There were some odd experiences, like meeting a casting director and offering to shake his hand, and him responding with a shriek: "No hands please, no hands!" Just crazy. Finally I called my manager and told him I couldn't do it any more.

A few weeks later, I started to write both a book and a movie script; things I would never have done here because I'd think, *I'm an actress, I can't write a book!* But over there, everybody's so insanely supportive. If I said, "I'm starting a cow's milk factory", they'd say, "Great, do it!"

Here, people would tell you every reason why it's dumb. Obviously, you need a middle ground, but the American attitude is quite liberating if you're creative. Everyone's writing something in LA – even the dentist will tell you he's writing a novel! Nobody ever seems to be working – they're all typing furiously in cafés and on terraces. So I just joined in and got started, living the American dream, writing my book. It was the first time I had the guts to try.

When I returned after a year, I threw the manuscript into the bin, but a friend of mine fished it out, showed a publisher and they liked it. I would never have done that, because the minute I got back, my Amsterdam-self started saying, *What on earth were you thinking?*

MY BIGGEST FEAR WAS CYCLING IN AMSTERDAM. I'D BEEN TOLD, "LOOK OUT FOR THE TRAM LINES, DON'T GET YOUR WHEEL STUCK IN THEM!"

A prominent reviewer at the *Volkskrant* newspaper once wrote that I should quit the TV programme that I appear in and stop with the movies; I should just prove my talent within the four walls of the theatre and end all this red carpet stuff. That's how it can be in Holland – "Stay where you are, don't become famous" – although that can also be a good thing, in contrast to other countries. In Tokyo, you're almost revered as a goddess! The Americans are always crying and shouting, "Oh my God, your show's so unbelievable!" The Germans are very intellectual; they want to discuss the theme of the play, and they're very well educated about the arts.

Of all the cities I've seen, though, I prefer to live here; not just because of my friends, but because it's healthier for me. The attitudes here keep you connected, grounded. Maybe I will live elsewhere for a year, and I do go away for months when I make a movie, but I will always return. I suppose if I have any children – don't know if I will, but if I do – I'll need a lot more money to survive here, because I wouldn't like my child to grow up in a tiny apartment. There is a high premium for living in this city, but we pay the premium because we love the place.

I hesitated about buying a home here, because I was travelling all over the place. Now that I've bought it, I feel much more peaceful in myself. Even after being here for so many years, I still have moments when I walk through the streets at night and think, *Wow, it's so beautiful here!* The old houses across my street look like a museum and I love that. Friends of mine have an apartment near the Anne Frank House, and some tourists think they're extras in the museum, acting out that they are living there!

Halina has performed in most venues in Amsterdam. Every member of the public has his or her favourite, but I think it's interesting to ask which locations the actors enjoy most.

When I was just 11 years old, my Groningen theatre group came to Amsterdam to play at a beautiful theatre called De Brakke Grond. We went on to have a look at the Stadsschouwburg [one of the city's main theatres] on Leidseplein and it all made such a massive impression on me. I looked up at the building and dreamed, *One day I will be on stage here...* After I arrived in Amsterdam, I joined a group called De Trust, and they were based on the Kloveniersburgwal. That theatre was special, because it was so small and intimate, with only around 400 seats – it's still there.

Even so, I must admit that I'm still in love with the Stadsschouwburg. We have two theatres there: the beautiful old-fashioned hall, and a more modern one called the Rabozaal that's completely different. The windows are huge, so we often have a crowd outside on the Melkweg side, looking in and watching us rehearse. We like that; we want to be involved with the city, to be in contact with the public of Amsterdam, whatever their nationality – that's why we show surtitles in English now, so that we attract visitors and expats, as well as locals.

The theatre company I belong to, Toneelgroep Amsterdam, is a really important part of my life. It might have been possible to have a bigger movie career if I'd focused solely on films, but I made a conscious decision to develop myself within this group, because I love it. The 22 actors and the director are at the highest level possible.

We move from the mezzanine into the lovely old film theatre, with its plush red seats and classic décor. Halina is in her element because Joost is shooting portrait photographs of her – and for once she's not obliged to talk about her 'latest project'.

It's enjoyable to talk about the city. I mean, you work on something for a long time and after it's finished, you have to talk about it for ages. Many interviews switch very quickly to the same old stories: "Do you have a boyfriend, and are you going to have any children?"

Bret Easton Ellis was here a couple of weeks ago for a book tour and a group of us went out for dinner with him. He was very depressed about the tour, saying, "I'm *so* over this book, I can't talk about it any more." He was amazing though. As soon as he was being interviewed, he did it so well, telling jokes, making the show interesting. You have to do it, but it can be tiring.

A big moment comes for me when Halina takes the time to pose for a shot while holding my first book. She's another accomplished person from The Essence™ who recognises someone trying to start something new and respects it. To close, we talk about what she would change about Amsterdam if she could.

I would change the shops! The clothes you can buy here are not good for me. The fanciest shopping street, PC Hooftstraat, is totally influenced by footballers' wives! I only buy clothes in other countries. If you want to spend money on clothes, it's difficult here – unless you're a soccer player's wife. But if you have any taste, well, think again...

Leidseplein could be different too. There are so many trams, taxis and buses around that area and I would prefer it if the space was kept for people to walk around and enjoy. It should be for strolling to the theatre and sitting in cafés, not for cars. Still, it's my favourite place in the city.

www.halinareijn.nl

SPIEGELSTRAAT

Spiegel is the Dutch word for mirror. Someone who asks Amsterdam to look into the mirror and question itself is anonymous street artist Laser 3.14.

YOU CAN'T EMULATE AN AMSTERDAM STREET IN A GALLERY

LASER 3.14

ANONYMOUS STREET AND GRAPHIC ARTIST

NO FURTHER INFO

Renovation is a recurring sight around Amsterdam's streets. A combination of natural renewal, a new metro line and a (successful) bid to be placed on UNESCO's World Heritage list are all factors in this. And where there's renovation, invariably there's a message from Laser 3.14.

For a few years now his tags have appealed to my fascination for wordplay; always a sentence in his familiar sprayed script, always a thought or emotion provoked. Graffiti can be an annoyance when it's on your front door, but Laser *adds* to the environment, rather than taking away from it.

In fact, it's almost as if a renovation isn't complete without a Laser 3.14 signature piece. His work has become a part of the architecture and landscape of Amsterdam.

I read a book about him and discovered that he keeps his identity hidden. More intrigue. I wanted to talk with him about his view of Amsterdam, but how do you get in contact with an anonymous street artist? Hang around a construction site long enough to find him at work, interrupt and ask, "Sorry to bother you, Laser – do I call you Laser? – but would you be interested in a chat?"

Even a secretive artist wants to showcase his work and sure enough, he has a website – with a contact email address.

I send him my introduction message and a 10-line summary of this book. In response, I receive the following:

From: callisto green
Subject: **Re: Interview?**
Date: May 10, 2010 4:01:35 PM GMT+02:00
To: David Beckett <david.beckett@theessenceonline.com>

Hi david
Thanks for your mail. I'm in.
Cheers
L314

Right. On the one hand, success. On the other – what happens next? And what's with the 'callisto green' address?

After more, similarly cryptic correspondence, we agree to meet at a café on a Saturday at lunchtime. However, I still don't know what he looks like. I wait outside and imagine each passer-by to be him. Is he the colourful, junkie-like hippie? No. The rapper hoody? Think again. The cute girl in the yellow T-shirt with 'Fuck Wilders' on it? Definitely not.

Finally, a very cool looking figure locks his bike on the corner of the street, strolls towards me and raises his eyebrows (unbeknownst to me, he's seen me before). With the slightest nod of the head, he indicates that I should go inside. We sit at the back of the café, and I'm face-to-face with my anonymous Amsterdam hero.

THIS CITY IS MY CANVAS!

Amsterdam is really my city. I do want to taste the essence of other cities and maybe live in London for a year, New York for a few months, but my home base will always be Amsterdam.

Of course, when you're young, you get a bit discontented and think about leaving, but now I feel rooted here. It's the carefree style and the openness; I really like the freedom we have. Compare it with any city in the world and it's unique. The best part is that there are lots of different cultures living together – seemingly without problems. Well, that is changing a bit, but when I grew up there was hardly any racism. My friends were Italian, Surinamese, Yugoslavian, and we weren't concerned about this colour or that colour, this country or that country – we were just names and people, nothing beyond that.

I'd expected a hardened, cynical kind of guy because some of Laser's tags are very confrontational, yet in the first seconds of our talk, it's clear that he's a personable, calmly spoken and sensitive guy. He talks avidly about both his graphic and street art.

It's a conscious decision to keep the two separate. When my street work began to be noticed, I tried to fuse the two styles but they didn't connect. That's still something I'm trying to figure out and it's fascinating to try to find a way.

Plenty of street artists use graphics, but I decided to keep the word-art out in the open and show the graphic art in galleries. Street work belongs in the street. There are so many elements around you while you're looking at it; light, wind, sound, temperature, passers-by. All the senses are involved and you can't replicate that in a gallery, which is quiet and static. Street art is universal, because anyone can see it as they walk around Amsterdam. They don't have to go to a gallery; they can see my work on their way to the office or shops.

I'm a big fan of Jean Giraud, who has a second persona as the artist Moebius. The two identities create completely separate strands of art and for years I didn't know it was the same guy. Once I found out, it made me realise it's possible to develop two very different artistic

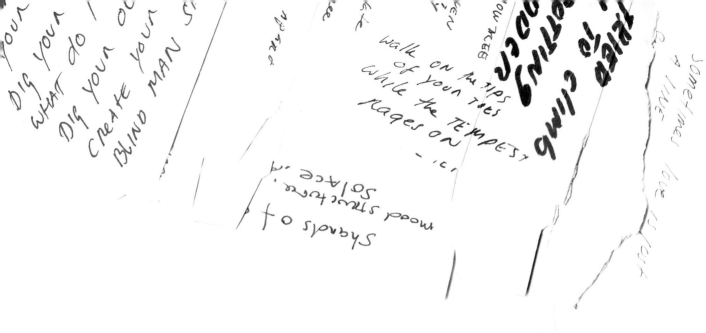

forms and not have them interfere with each other.

I'll continue with both these tracks of art as long as I can work with the same creative fire. The moment that diminishes, it's time to stop. Otherwise the art becomes lame and the quality declines. For now, I'm still having so much fun and have many ideas to work with. Sometimes the two art forms influence each other – I might come to a small 'block' with the graphic art, and the word-art will help free my mind up to flow again.

The tags always come as one complete piece and I don't try to adjust or edit them in case I change the original emotion of the writing. It's very important for me that the emotions are pure and the work exactly reflects how I feel at that very moment. I have this huge pile of notes that has developed over time, because when I get an idea, I need to scribble it down before it's gone. Sometimes an idea lies in the pile for years and now and again I go through the notes to see if anything has become relevant.

Cycling to the interview, I'd seen a tag on a sheet of material wrapped around some scaffolding, at a renovation on Spuistraat. His words were at fourth floor level, upside down. How on earth did he do that?

I saw that! It wasn't planned to be so high-up. I wrote it at ground level, but I guess the material got re-used for another renovation and suddenly I find the work in a different place. That kind of thing happens a lot. Sometimes I might tag across two pieces of builder's board blocking over a window and later the builders will put the pieces in different places, leaving my words mixed up, or a half-sentence behind. I love that because the message becomes even more surprising, almost by accident. It turns into something dynamic, just like the city.

Most of my friends are a bit frustrated with all the renovation around Amsterdam, but for Laser, it's perfect.

This city is my canvas! Every day I develop new ideas for pieces and find new locations for my work – we live in a renovation city.

Part of the appeal of what I do is the element of surprise. You're on your way to work and walk around the corner only to find my piece – and the next day it could be gone. Sometimes I get posterised very quickly, but I prefer the 'here today, gone tomorrow' effect. It's part of the ever-changing, ever-evolving city and a fundamental aspect of the art. It's nice to know it's there for a fixed period, but that period could be a day, two days, a week. Then again, sometimes I turn a corner and find something I wrote five years ago, and think, *That's cool! It's still around.* I know those words on the board have travelled to different renovations around the city, gone through some hard winters, but the art has lasted.

Some of Laser's tags are highly political and I wonder how conscious that is as an approach. I'm also interested to know what he thinks of the current status of Amsterdam's famed tolerance.

My work has become increasingly influenced by politics. That wasn't the case when I started, around 10 years ago, but these days I am very political as a person and that shows in my tags. It's good to use street art to share a message – because it's so open to everyone, so you can provoke the public into thinking about wider issues.

It's hard *not* to be political as an artist in Amsterdam. I feel we've been terrorised by political correctness in the past 15 years, which can have serious consequences for the city. There are a few conservative individuals in power who want to close down the Red Light District [RLD] and the coffee shops. That might look better cosmetically, but the original reasons for allowing prostitution and soft drugs were about bringing these social issues out from the shadows and enabling a certain amount of regulation.

Let's say you close some red light windows down; the girls will get into trouble because they won't be out in the open any more, and instead will end up in some rough room in a back street with no rights or protection. The authorities should wage war against the criminal aspect of that area, for sure, but I believe an open society is always better than a repressive one. If you close the district down,

IT'S PART OF THE EVER-CHANGING, EVER-EVOLVING CITY

you simply move the problem back into the shadows.

Amsterdam's authorities have taken too much notice of a few whining complaints from new inhabitants who came for a quiet life, rather than embracing the living spirit of the city. The danger is that it becomes really difficult to compete with other world cities. They're putting too many rules onto a place that used to have hardly any rules and hardly any problems!

There's a religious aspect too. People whose fundamental values are not about freedom of life and speech are coming to live in the Netherlands. I know it takes time for cultures to adapt and integrate, but there is a danger of us being too tolerant of intolerance. Those who come to live here have to respect the core values of tolerance and we shouldn't accept it if they don't.

New directives are coming for the coffee shops, and this seems pointless to me. You can easily argue that marijuana is much less dangerous than alcohol. Take the number of accidents and violence as a result of alcohol and compare it with marijuana, and anyone can see that alcohol is a hundred times more dangerous! I think marijuana should be legalised, with a sensible age limit, maybe 20 years old. Amsterdam makes money from it, as well as from the RLD – closing coffee shops and prostitute windows down in order to appear politically correct is negative for the city's economy.

I love the city and feel I have to make a statement when I see things going in a direction against our history. Rembrandt is fucking buried here, Spinoza was really important for Amsterdam – doesn't that tell us something about honouring a legacy of creativity and freethinking?

A mint tea arrives for Laser, a large hot chocolate brimming with cream for me. The contrast is a touch embarrassing. I can't tell you much about Laser as I have agreed to keep his identity secret – but I can at least say he seems a healthy guy who works out.

Inevitably we begin talking about his anonymity and whether it's a practical decision or related to his intentions as an artist. With some hesitation, I raise the possibility that Laser was influenced into anonymity by the success of English street artist Banksy.

Of course I know of him, but it's just coincidence. While he was becoming famous, I was developing my graphic work and had no real connection to the street art world. When I started doing the sentences, I made the decision to take the identity of Laser 3.14. Two or three years later, a friend showed me some of Banksy's stuff – I thought it was interesting! Nevertheless, my work and decision to be anonymous are unrelated to him.

What I do is technically illegal, because you can't apply paint on any surface in the city – even though I try to add to the environment by doing my work where there is some chaos already. But my anonymity is basically because of the art. I want to stay in the background and let my work speak for itself.

I've seen some artists sitting next to their pieces, being photographed while talking about them. For me, that takes the power away, because often they over-explain. They can look like used-car salesmen! I've decided to avoid my discontent with that. Some artists can be brilliant at explanation and are characters in themselves, but I don't see myself that way.

Mystery has always been special for me. Growing up, my kid brother and I used to listen to pirate radio a lot, and we loved the new rap music that was developing in the '80s. We didn't know anything about how these guys looked and that made it even more powerful. You start imagining, *These guys in New York, where are they from? How old are they? What do they wear?* I find the effect much stronger if your own imagination is brought into play and that's why I decided to include that into my own approach to art.

The 3.14 part of my pseudonym is a reference to a 45-inch single I bought years ago by the band Public Image Limited - the B-side was simply called *Public Image*. I took the mathematical idea that the initials of that song make up as the concept behind my persona.

At this stage I admit to Laser that I'd expected him to be much more hard-nosed.

Well, sometimes you *do* have to grab the audience by the balls. I like subtlety, but at times you have to be clear and direct. Some will like it and some won't, and you can't focus on those who don't like it. At some stage in the development of my work, I decided: *I will not compromise on anything.* Compromise means you can't create as your real self. I'm human – cynical at times, but I am also in a lovey-dovey phase sometimes and then I write about that.

Not compromising is difficult. Amsterdam is full of struggling artists doing what they do, and we probably all feel the same way at some stage about not following a 'normal' path. I did have a good job at the end of the '90s, in a print shop, which paid pretty well – but I hated it! After one and a half years I'd had enough. It was totally non-artistic and I needed to get my creativity back.

I left the job and got really poor. I didn't have *any* money for a couple of years, but I was so happy going out on the street and doing my tags. I said to my mother, "That's the only thing I want to do, make my art." Naturally she wanted me to get a job, but she came round to the idea and supported my decision.

These days I get commissions for different kinds of creative work, like *De Laatste Dichters* [The Last Poets]. It's a stage show and they wanted some graffiti in the background, so I did a series of tags for the set and for promotional material. That gig came as a result of my street art.

Another 'Amsterdam creates opportunities' story lies behind Laser's book *Are You Reading Me?*

After a couple of years of street-writing, I had a collection of photographs and thought a book was a logical next step. I made a dummy and sent it to a lot of publishers, but most of them refused me or I never heard anything back from them. Then I met Rick Lightstone from the American Book Centre in Amsterdam, who told me, "I know a lot of publishers, but I don't know much about street art, so I don't know if your book is going to sell."

We agreed to put a dummy in the shop with a 'not for sale' sticker on it. After displaying it on a Friday, he called me the following Monday to tell me that customers had been picking it up to browse through, and many wanted to buy it immediately. So we went ahead, found a publisher and produced it. The final version ended up looking totally different to the dummy, which was A4, a black page with a poem on one side, a street-tag photo on the other. It was very stylish, but we came to the conclusion that we shouldn't use poetry because it confused people, making them ask, "Is this a poetry or street art book?" The poetry detracted from the photos.

Finally we reached the idea to make the theme of the book more about Amsterdam and the location of the tags; the surroundings and environment, the atmosphere of the city. I'm proud of the final result.

What's the essence of Amsterdam? I have the freedom to be who I want to be here. I don't have a lot of people telling me how to be, or if they do, I don't have to listen! Not sure if that's *the* essence but it is *my* essence.

www.laser314.com

Regularly voted as the most beautiful street in the Netherlands, it runs along the end of Amsterdam's three main canals. Paul Spies is a specialist in the history of the development of the famous canal circle.

THE HISTORICAL ESSENCE OF AMSTERDAM? FREE THINKING, CREATIVITY, ENTREPRENEURSHIP, CITIZENSHIP

PAUL SPIES

AMSTERDAMMER SINCE 1960
ART HISTORIAN AND SPECIALIST ON AMSTERDAM'S GIRDLE OF CANALS
FAVOURITE AMSTERDAM LOCATION – BROUWERSGRACHT, ON THE CORNER OF HERENGRACHT

To understand any country or city, some knowledge of its history is probably helpful. Nevertheless, not many of us – and least of all me, having given up history at the earliest opportunity at school – really want to trawl page after page of some dry listing of dates and dignitaries.

The Amsterdam Museum formerly had 'historical' attached to its name, but its Director, Paul Spies, moved to change this when he became its head. His ambition was for visitors to come through the main exhibition in the museum to get a good overview of his city's recent and not-so-recent history in just 45 minutes. Naturally they could stay longer and go in depth, but if not, at least they'd have received a basic historical overview before going on to explore the canals and streets.

Paul's passion for sharing knowledge and my inability to concentrate on written history worked surprisingly well together. He effortlessly intrigued me with his explanation of the four kinds of light around the *grachtengordel* [girdle of canals around the old city], and kept my attention with his descriptions of it as the ultimate democratic construction.

It's a gift to be able to tell history as a story, and Paul has that talent. Thanks to him, I'm now beginning to understand the underlying reasons for my home town's famed tolerance and openness, qualities originating in the middle of the last millennium.

So read on, and next time you go for a bike ride along the canals, you'll know why they are so special. It's quite a story...

Having the *grachtengordel* listed by UNESCO World Heritage is a significant milestone for the city, something that's been worked on for over two decades. All that work has come to fruition at the right moment, because a very important date is coming up in 2013. It will be the 400th anniversary of the beginning of development of the canal circle, and we are planning a big commemoration.

It's incredible, isn't it? People abroad regard Amsterdam primarily as a 'canal city', like Venice, yet there has been little information available about the grachtengordel other than on the boat trips. Three million take those boat tours every year, but there are very few buildings around the waters that you can enter to get a deeper sense of their history. We want to improve that for the commemoration year.

One of the first things I did on arriving in Amsterdam was to enjoy the stunning views and atmosphere of the three main waterways: Keizersgracht, Herengracht and Prinsengracht. I imagined there was a grand plan behind the design.

It's naturally assumed that the pattern of the canals was created to make the city beautiful, but I have to stress that the *grachtengordel* was designed for practical reasons, as a communal concept. It brought together a very diverse community of people.

Trade was the most important reason for waterways throughout the city. Everything naturally went by boat in Holland, therefore traders wanted their goods to be loaded or unloaded directly at their houses. A merchant would store his goods on the top floor of his house and sell them at street level.

Without a monarch, who might have wanted a Roman-style layout as happened in other major European cities, the development authorities could make pragmatic decisions. The city centre already had a half-moon form at the water's edge so they made the crescent shape surround the centre. Canals were dug to radiate away from fortifications along the water designed to repel potential invasions by the Spanish and French.

This trade-focused plan had an influence on the then homogeneous society of Amsterdam. There were many rich families around the year 1600, but also a new developing class of merchant traders who had some money – and were working like crazy to make more.

Richer inhabitants lived in the canal houses, while the backstreets were used for the coach houses and servants' quarters. So, if you were rich, your house backed onto places where the poorer people lived. The shops and craftspeople used the streets that crossed all the canals; the Jordaan was the industrial area where the working people set up home. The different groups would meet each other in the streets and in church and got to know each other as a result.

Was it planned that this construction would contribute to our tolerance, or was it just an outcome? You know, everything in Amsterdam is an outcome!

In the 19th century, everyone was looking for the brilliant architect behind the design of the canals, yet they couldn't find him. Finally they had to accept there was no architect – just an opportunity and circumstances which made this construction the most logical.

If you're lucky enough to see the canals on a sunny day, Paul has something for you to think about: four kinds of light.

One architect, Berlage, praised the beauty of the canals, and tried to analyse it. He concluded that it's partly because there is a rhythm and consistency to the combination of buildings and water, even though each house is different. This beauty comes from the constant curve of the water and the streets alongside it. If the canals were straight, you would have a distant horizon, but the curves cause the close horizon to change constantly as you walk. Varying light is key too, and you can make a comparison with New York. There, the sun comes from the side and you have enormous long streets – also very interesting – but the sun is constantly coming from the same place as you walk in one direction. In Amsterdam, nothing is straight.

There are always trees by the canals too; light is filtered through the leaves, creating continuous movement and play. A constant wind also moves the leaves so the light is always changing. The trees are Dutch elms, which have a resin and shine to them, and that reflects the sunshine. Also, the water reflects the light in a continually changing pattern.

On top of all this, the gables of each house are at slightly different heights, so the light is again changing as you move around the canal circle. On a dark day, the canals are attractive, but it's not the same as on a sunny day when the light is doing so many different things all at once.

So what does Paul consider to be the essence of Amsterdam? Unlike many, who scratch their head when asked, struggling to define it, Paul's face lights up as he says, "I know that!" He reaches for the yearbook of the museum and on the back of the golden book are four Dutch words...

Firstly you have *vrijdenken* – free thinking. This is the basis for all aspects of the city development and it came from water being the common enemy that bound Hollanders together. You couldn't spend too much time deciding whether you liked your neighbour or not; you had to get on and work together regardless. I believe our famed tolerance comes from this. Some would say it was forced tolerance, not by choice, and they could be right.

Then you have *ondernemerschap*, meaning entrepreneurship. The concept of shares and trading originated in Holland and the voyages to the Spice Islands were financed by risk-taking groups of entrepreneurs. The 'start-up' business culture is still very strong here, and that relies too on *creativiteit*, or creativity. Finally, you have *burgerschap*, which you could translate as being a member and a part of the city, contributing to it.

These four concepts are interlinked. That combination is surely the essence of Amsterdam.

www.amsterdammuseum.nl

AS AN AMSTERDAMMER, YOU SHOULD ENJOY YOUR FREEDOM, AND BE READY TO DEFEND IT FOR OTHERS — EVEN IF THEY ARE DIFFERENT

AHMED MARCOUCH

AMSTERDAMMER SINCE 1979
MEMBER OF DUTCH PARLIAMENT
FAVOURITE AMSTERDAM LOCATION — CANAL CIRCLE [GRACHTENGORDEL]

On a Sunday afternoon in summer 2010, hundreds joined together to make a statement against violence towards gay people. I had never been on a protest before, but this cause touched me because two of my best friends had experienced prejudice in the past.

As the protesters gathered at the Homomonument next to the Westerkerk, a series of speeches were made by prominent figures from, or supporting, the Amsterdam gay community, including the organiser, Fya Hopelezz [see interview on page 110]. To my great surprise, one of those speakers was a shaven-headed Moroccan guy.

A friend told me, "That's Ahmed Marcouch. He's a Muslim who stands up for gay rights. You should interview him for your book as he has a very different view of Amsterdam."

Very impressive, I thought. Here's a man taking a difficult position. Still, I hesitated. I had already interviewed one labour party politician, Job Cohen [see page 126], and I didn't want to be seen as favouring a particular party, especially as I had little knowledge of Dutch politics.

"Don't talk to him about politics," my friend "Just ask him what he thinks. Marcouch is one of those characters from the city who don't follow what people expect of them."

A few months later, I made my way to the Dutch houses of parliament and found a charming and charismatic man. He was a little delayed and I expected our time slot to be shortened accordingly, but Marcouch ensured he kept his promise by rearranging his meetings so that we had enough time to talk.

He then enlightened me on what the common image of freedom in Amsterdam really means.

I was 10 years old when my father brought our family to Amsterdam from Morocco. He'd arrived some years earlier, when there was a big demand for *gastarbeiders* [guest or immigrant workers], and we had a chance to become Dutch citizens. The Netherlands seemed very exotic to us, because my father looked so different to everyone else on his visits home to Morocco, smelling of aftershave and wearing unusual clothing.

It was such a surprise arriving in the Netherlands, because we had been living in a rural village with little infrastructure – no TV, no schools, very few cars and rough roads. When we were driven by taxi to the airport from our village, those 30 kilometres felt like 300, it was so bumpy! Flying was the first miracle, and when we saw the Dutch houses and the way the roads were shiny instead of dusty, we couldn't believe our eyes. I kept tripping on the stairs of our house, because I wasn't used to walking up or down them.

Never having been to school, I was illiterate, so my first confrontation with Amsterdam life was learning how to communicate. In Morocco I had really wanted to go to school and when I was given that opportunity in Amsterdam, I began studying the Dutch language with all my energy, in the same way I had memorised the Koran texts in Morocco. I developed my vocabulary by reading out loud, which was the only way I knew – the whole idea of reading quietly was unknown to me then. Within a couple of years I was pretty fluent.

Amsterdam was the first city I had lived in, and it was very difficult to begin with. We stayed in a small apartment with just one room for our family of six. At night we would divide it in two with a curtain, turning it into a living room and a bedroom. The beds were lined up right next to each other.

Our apartment was in the east of the city, near what my father called 'market 3' – Dappermarkt. Many immigrants couldn't pronounce Dutch words and had come up with a system for Amsterdam markets, naming them with a number according to the nearest tram. Albert Cuypmarkt was number 16, Ten Katemarkt was market 17, and so on. Being in a strange place can make you very creative.

Marcouch faces challenges around the issue of identity, having left his home country when he was so young.

Defining my nationality is difficult. I have lived in this city for three quarters of my life and that means I am 'Dutchified'. I know the Moroccan culture and language very well, but when I go back, I don't feel very Moroccan. I certainly think I'm an Amsterdammer in many respects. This is my first and only city and I had only worked in Amsterdam, until my new job in Den Haag; it feels almost as if I'm in exile now...

A warm grin spreads across his face, and widens when I ask, "Would you ever live in Den Haag?" He answers with a firm "No!" Perhaps this is more representative of the natural friction between a capital and other cities, than of any weakness of Den Haag itself.

Other parts of Holland are beautiful. I do notice, when I'm in the south of the Netherlands, like Limburg, or in the north, like Friesland, that there's still a bit of that country boy in me. I get a nostalgic feeling; that maybe I would like to live on a small farm with quiet surroundings. A lot of my friends first lived in Amsterdam, but they couldn't afford a house with a garden, so they left for Almere and Purmerend. I have thought about it, because I'd also like to have a house like that, but the idea of leaving Amsterdam to go and live in a new city... No, I don't think I'll ever leave.

Ten years as an Amsterdam policeman was the basis for Marcouch's move into politics.

In my police work, I often considered the difficulties that came along with changes in neighbourhoods, as a lot of new nationalities started moving in. I felt the politicians didn't have an answer to those developments. They based their plans on sparse information, from one or two members of those new communities, which I felt was insufficient.

Some years ago, I took the opportunity to work at the council on a strategic project, as a co-ordinator for youth and safety, because that way I thought my ideas might finally be heard. That led to me being asked by the PvdA [Labour Party] to be party leader for my area in the west of the city, Slotervaart, and I went on to become chairman of the district.

My police experience, together with being a migrant's child, helped me a lot in my role. There was a period as a teenager when I became very radical as a Muslim. It was part of my development and as I grew into Amsterdam as my home and the Netherlands as my society, I changed my view. From having focused on the decadence of the people and seeing the situation as 'them and us', I started to see the beauty of the city's freedom and safety.

The essence of our Amsterdam society, more than any other city, is freedom. And freedom can only exist if you take responsibility and defend it as a principle – even for others who might be very different to you. For example, Muslims should fight for the right to wear a headscarf, but should also be prepared to support the freedom of someone who doesn't want to, and not force them to.

This also applies to gay rights. Once an orthodox Muslim attacked me for supporting gay rights, but my answer was this: "Your freedom as a Muslim to walk around Amsterdam with traditional Islamic clothing, to have your mosque with a minaret here – perhaps that's something you simply expect. In truth, it's an achievement that you can do those things in a completely different country to your own. That freedom is exactly the same freedom of the gay person. The moment you touch their rights, you are scraping away at the basis of your own freedom."

I want to help the public become aware of what the essence of living together really is. A major part of it is safety; you can't be free if you don't feel safe. It's a sense of being welcome, of being allowed to express who you really are. I believe too many politicians want to deal with this simply with a law, when we should be doing more than just making laws. Leadership is about creating a vision; about drawing a picture of the future to help make others aware of the core values of the city. Only once the vision is established should the politicians and the citizens try to arrange the necessary details to shape that story. Politics is more than just law-making or dividing budgets.

When Marcouch talks about freedom, there is a startling clarity in his eyes. His whole demeanour shows how important a subject this is for him, even though it may have caused him some difficulties among a section of his own Moroccan community.

Some have turned on me for this, but I always say I'm not going to bargain when it comes to something as fundamental as the freedom to be who you are. I can't tell a gay person, "Sorry, you're living in Amsterdam, where a lot of Muslims think you should behave differently." That's not an option.

The security to be visible as who you are must be an essential part of Amsterdam life. A Muslim can wear signs of his faith and that's something to be proud of. In the same instant, I want to be proud of the fact that a gay person can be openly gay here. Of course this is not always popular with the Moroccan community – but I've also made many pleas for Muslim rights.

I was the first politician who dared to say we should have room for orthodoxy, because that's also a part of our civilisation and city. I'm not an advocate of orthodox people *per se*, but when someone's orthodox within the boundaries of the law, I believe it should be allowed. The error that many make is in thinking you are not religious if you defend a person's right to something that is against your own belief. I consider my faith to be a private identity. Many say, "You can't stand up for them because it contradicts your religion." I don't experience any conflict though, because I stand up for something essential, for basic human rights.

Marcouch cycles through the city and takes the tram, just like everyone else. He has striking features and is instantly recognisable, which draws reactions from passers-by.

Sometimes they just watch you to see how you behave, other times they approach with a nice comment. Occasionally, I get shouted at from a distance, "*Hoi*, homo! Traitor!"

It's good to travel the same way as everybody else, you gain a better feeling about the daily life of those you represent. I take the train every day, which means that I sometimes have to hear someone's story when I just want to read – but I always learn something.

During the years, I've developed an emotion for the city. When I walk through the canals, especially in the morning when it's spring weather and there's a bit of sunshine, I almost feel nostalgic for the Golden Age, when the canals were developed. You realise that, centuries ago, other people were walking here, in a completely different context, yet so much is the same. I find the historical city incredibly impressive. You can almost hear the walls talking to you.

www.ahmedmarcouch.nl

Diverse market stalls appear here every Monday and Saturday. And as it's just a few blocks away from her favourite area, you might just bump into the striking figure of Mariette Hoitink.

THE VOICE OF THE PEOPLE IS IMPORTANT HERE. IT IS TYPICAL AMSTERDAM TO HAVE "HET HART OP DE TONG." WHATEVER YOU FEEL, JUST SAY IT

MARIETTE HOITINK

AMSTERDAMMER SINCE 1988
MANAGING DIRECTOR OF HTNK FASHION RECRUITMENT AND CONSULTANCY
FAVOURITE AMSTERDAM LOCATIONS — WESTERPARK AND WESTERGASFABRIEK

A spirit of commerce is part of Amsterdam's history, and in modern times the city maintains a strong business start-up culture.

The famed tolerance of the Netherlands, and in its capital in particular, has always been a practical attitude towards encouraging commerce. A small nation with big ambitions, the Dutch realised early on that they would need to co-operate with other nationalities and cultures to succeed.

Some simple examples: the ships that the British sent to the Spice Islands in the 16th century were predominantly manned by British sailors, whereas those sent by the Dutch were crewed by sailors from around the globe. And at a time when Catholics were being burned at the stake in much of Europe, Amsterdam became a safe haven for most religions. If you could work and bring money in, you were welcome.

Today, entrepreneurship is at the heart of Amsterdam. It's a place where you feel you can create something and make a difference. If you have enough drive and belief, it seems you can do anything.

Mariette Hoitink is one of those Amsterdammers who maintains this age-old spirit in everything she does. Ambitious and focused, she revels in the contrasts of world business travel and the smaller, simpler life of Amsterdam's Haarlemmerdijk and Bickerseiland.

That drive and focus has helped Mariette build an amazing career. She not only established HTNK as a premier fashion recruitment and consultancy agency, but has also been the driving force behind the revolutionary Redlight Fashion Amsterdam project, as well as numerous other development events for designers and labels alike.

I arrive at her very stylish office on the edge of the Red Light District, and instead of sitting in a fancy office, we sit in the kitchen. "I would really like to eat a herring," she says. "Do you like them?"

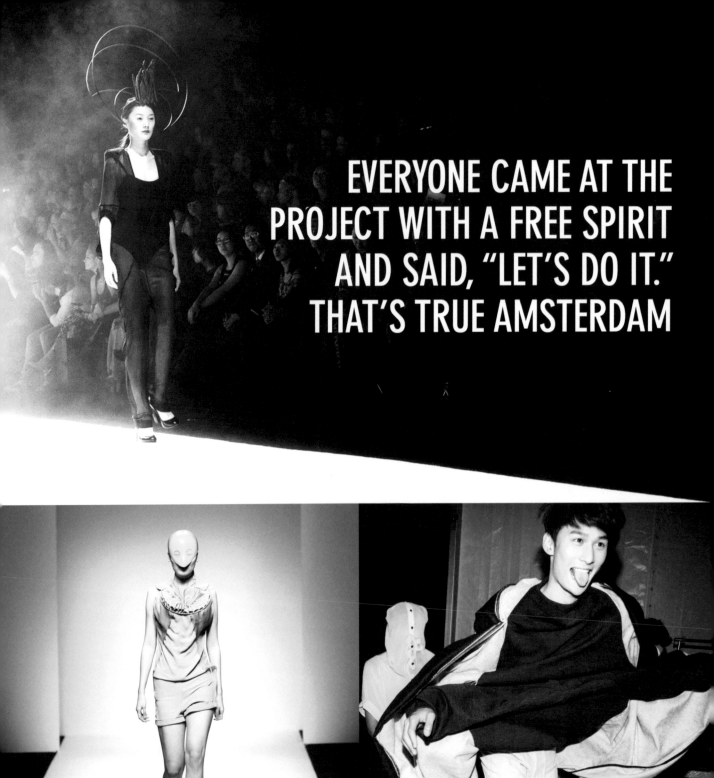

EVERYONE CAME AT THE PROJECT WITH A FREE SPIRIT AND SAID, "LET'S DO IT." THAT'S TRUE AMSTERDAM

I studied and graduated in fashion design in the '80s. At that time, it wasn't something your parents would be positive about, because it was difficult to find work in that field, but my brother, sister and I were brought up to be individuals. We were supported, not pressured, to do our own thing.

While working as a buyer for a clothing retailer, I travelled the world. Within two years, I was head of their department and had to do presentations, also to other international stores in the chain, such as El Corte Inglés in Spain and Karstadt in Germany. I was very young and nervous as hell at times, but I learned by being out there. On one occasion I had to give a presentation in German, and I only found this out the day before! My German was not very good, but I memorised every word and practised all night. Even now I can tell you exactly what was in that presentation!

Hardly surprising. Mariette immediately shows herself to be the kind of person who doesn't say, "I can't do it" but rather asks, "How can I do it?" This attitude enabled her to see a gap in the fashion industry.

When I was working for big companies, I was headhunted many times, but I didn't like their approach. They always seemed to think I was just a dollar sign; they never took the time to understand me as a person, or what I wanted.

After one trip to India, I returned with all kinds of bacteria in my body and was very ill for some months. Overnight, I stopped working so that I could recover and this gave me time to think about what I wanted to do. I found myself looking back on those headhunting experiences and decided to set up a recruitment agency [called HTNK] to work in the way that I wanted to be headhunted; that is, to build relationships and get to know the individual.

I had a big network. I hate that word, when I hear talk of going to an event "to improve their network" – but it's true, I had contacts with all the major retailers, as well as with a lot of designers and creative people. I set up the company and created the connections between them, and HTNK grew from that basis. It's satisfying to create a team, to be the glue between others.

Side by side with the agency work, Mariette and her team invest time to help creatives who want to establish their own labels. She gets carried away by her story, as she talks about her passion for connecting designers with business.

Getting design graduates into a job is one thing, but helping them set up their own label straight from the academy is another. They lack the experience, networks and commercial skills to become entrepreneurs.

We created a workshop programme – in partnership with Syntens, the Dutch Fashion Foundation [DFF] and Arnhem Mode Biennale – called *Turning Talent Into Business*. When designers follow their studies, they are only surrounded by like-minded people, but later,

in business, they have to deal with those who use the other side of their brain. Designers often don't know how to deal with this, because they're in this whole creative field and just don't come into contact with accountants or marketeers. We want to help them with that.

To be chosen for the programme, a designer needs to have some kind of business plan and show their dedication by having worked in the industry for at least a year. We work with them to improve their plans. Our part of this project is also to connect the designers with anyone in our network that could be interesting for them.

HTNK also initiated the DUTCH FASHION HERE & NOW [DFH&N] programme, which aims to create awareness of the Dutch fashion identity in emerging countries. We show the best qualities of academy graduates as well as some established designers, and that helps create business opportunities for participating academies and designers. It also lays the ground for future Dutch fashion entrepreneurs. DFH&N was part of the Shanghai Fashion Week and the plan is to expand to India next.

Discussions about "Art for Art's Sake" are age-old. Mariette is a businesswoman first and foremost, who focuses on enabling creative people to survive in the commercial world.

In the end, whether you like it or not, as an artist, it has to become commercial if you want others to see your work. You can also live on the breadline, and just do your art without any recognition. In Holland and especially in Amsterdam, you can do whatever you want, but generally most artists do want their work to be visible. I don't like to hear comments about creatives 'selling out', just because they become successful. Marcel Wanders is an example; some say, "He's so commercial", but probably that comes from those who envy his ingenuity. Watch one of his presentations in Hong Kong or Japan or America; he blows everyone away!

The most creative designer in the world can never do business alone. Either they should find a good, reliable partner, or work in a company and spend their time doing what they are good at.

Development projects, and successful designers like Marcel, are good for Amsterdam's image. These days you have design tourists coming and spending money here, also thanks to the changes in the Red Light District [RLD]. It's good for the city; better than attracting the Brits who just come to buy beer or dope!

Perhaps the most controversial undertaking Mariette has been involved in is the Redlight Fashion Amsterdam project. I've heard numerous opinions about it from other Amsterdammers – both positive and negative. Mariette gives a very clear description of her involvement and of why the project is important for the city.

By chance, two guys from the city municipality came to my office, which is on the edge of the RLD. They explained the plan to take over some buildings in the area, together with the housing corporation, because the city aimed to clean up criminality. The owners wanted to sell immediately and the municipality hadn't decided what to do with the prostitute rooms in those buildings yet.

I said, "I know what to do!" I told them about this group of designers who have their own label and are part of *Turning Talent into Business*, and how they all share the same problem – nowhere prominent to show their work without having to pay a lot of money. Some of the designers were even quite successful already, but success and a full bank account are not the same. Starting up a business is especially difficult in high-end fashion, where the investments necessary to start a label are high and breaking even can take a long time.

My proposal was that they would get space for one year, where they could live and work for a lower rent than normal. That would enable the designers to focus their money on their collections – and having a shop window for the first time would be great for them and for the area.

Some months went by and then, out of the blue, those two guys came back and told me to go ahead with the plan – the opening would be in three weeks! So I called eighteen designers and told them, "You can get this place almost for free, but you have to decide now. I'll call you in the morning. Have an answer for me." Every single one agreed.

There was no pre-planning at all; we just went ahead and got started. This project was so typically Amsterdam – all the designers came at it with a free spirit and said, "Let's do it. I'm gonna get a van from a friend and get my stuff in." These people are nomads anyway, so they all moved in straight away, no problem!

Probably, if we'd made a big project plan it wouldn't have happened. It took three phone calls: to the mayor, the deputy mayor and the housing corporation, which owns the buildings. They all agreed, and we went for it.

I'm amazed so many were mobilised in such a short space of time to transform a chunk of the city's most iconic area into something new and modern. Yet I've often heard the opinion that this was the ultimate in 'gentrification', using artists to smarten up the area.

Naturally I understand it's controversial and that some think there's an element of exploitation of the artists, but it doesn't feel that way for the designers. They secured great locations to show their work to thousands, and Amsterdam gained the chance to show a different side of itself, not just hookers and drugs.

Once the story got out and we were ready to launch, it wasn't just the fashion press who came to hear about it. Suddenly the general press became involved too. The mayor announced the project and immediately there was an outcry: "They're going to shut down the Red Light District. Fashion's going to take over!" This was all over the Internet even before the opening.

The Amsterdam press office said, "There won't be much interest in the opening", but the day before the launch we had CNN, ABC and all the other big networks calling us. Then we realised, *Okay, it's going to be massive*. Perhaps we underestimated how powerful the image of Amsterdam is abroad.

The press value of this project was huge and the city realised this when the *International Herald Tribune* devoted a whole page to

it. I was interviewed about the project many times, so the whole neighbourhood knew I was behind it. When I was riding my bike, I'd get people shouting across the canal at me, "Redlight Fashion, what are you doing?" as if I have a personal goal to shut down the RLD! Yet all I did was exactly what I do in my agency: I put those with a need together with those who have something to offer. Nevertheless a lot of the locals thought, *Who are you working for?* The city must be telling you what to do. I can tell you, the authorities didn't tell me to do anything. *They* adapted to *my* idea.

It was positive that the city gave me the freedom to do what I wanted; there was no Q & A. From day one, we at HTNK decided to open it up, have the journalists here and explain the story. It was paparazzi time! Reporters wanted to get into these windows that were being used for the fashion displays, and we told them, "No problem, pay 50 euros to the girl in the room next door and you can get in; she also has to make a living."

The publicity turned the experience into a rollercoaster. It was never planned as a marketing tool to improve the RLD's image; it was just co-incidence that it took place here. If the opportunity had come up on the Haarlemmerdijk, I would have taken it, but it happened to be in this area that has so much interest for people and press.

The essence of the city *is* the Red Light District – you can feel the history in this area; you can imagine the VOC [Dutch East India Company] ships sailing into harbour, the sailors going to the pubs

and getting too drunk, going back with the ladies of pleasure, then straight to the Oude Kerk to confess their sins! It's a real place with a real history and I don't want the world to think of this area only as sex and drugs. This should be a place where many things are possible.

Opinions suggests this is the beginning of the end and it's often wondered what the RLD will be like in 20 years. Mariette shares her opinion with passion and confidence – as she does for all the subjects we touch on.

Well, it's certainly not going to be Gucci town! What I hope is that it will be full of new ideas and cutting-edge concepts of all kinds of cultural things; a nightclub, a bar, a restaurant, a shop, gallery, anything that is leading the way. This should be a zone that is *gedogen* [tolerated]. That concept is so typical of Amsterdam – it means something is not legal but it's permitted. This would ideally be the *gedoogde* zone, where things that aren't allowed in any other country can happen. It should be high and low level, chic as well as louche – not all fancy or just full of big brands, but also basic and down-to-earth. That is Amsterdam.

Mariette describes some of her favourite aspects of the city, and how the Amsterdammers' tendency to 'have an opinion' is not always to good effect.

The voice of the people is important in this city and that can be both a good thing and a bad thing. It is typical Amsterdam to have

'het hart op de tong' ['your heart on your tongue']; whatever you think or feel, just say it. For example, if I'm buying my herring on the corner, the guy next to me will be telling me how to vote. Everyone always has an opinion about everything. Sometimes I get fed up; sometimes you have to *do* something, not just state your opinion.

On the other hand, I can be who I want to be and do exactly what I want to do here in Amsterdam, and when I come back from travelling, being here feels like putting a warm jacket around me.

People don't care what you do or where you come from here – they judge you on who you are. In the USA, it's always about your standing. *You're a CEO? Okay, how many employees? Ah, over eleven, so you're something important...* I really don't care about these things, and neither do most Amsterdammers. They care about whether you are an interesting person and about how you get along with them, not status.

I hosted the mayor of Brooklyn here with his wife, and we met at Nieuwmarkt to take a tour around the city. I noticed they were a bit nervous, and as we were walking, the mayor said, "I'm amazed. I can walk here without any security! Treasure this – you don't know what you have!" It's at times like those you realise how lucky we are to live in Amsterdam.

www.htnk.nl
www.redlightfashionamsterdam.com
www.dutchfashionherenow.com

If you want to find the 'real old Amsterdam', this is the place. Peaceful narrow streets are dotted with markets, bars and restaurants. A lot of creative types hang out here too. That's why Def P does his work in the Jordaan.

AMSTERDAM'S CROOKED AND RAGGEDY - THAT'S WHY THE CITY'S GREAT TO PAINT

PASCAL GRIFFIOEN - AKA DEF P

BORN AND RAISED IN AMSTERDAM
MUSICIAN, WRITER, PLAYWRIGHT AND ARTIST
FAVOURITE AMSTERDAM LOCATION – MELKWEG MUSIC VENUE

My life in Amsterdam and the world of Dutch rap have rarely overlapped.

Until now.

Def P came recommended as a creative and intelligent guy, involved in all kinds of artistic pursuits. After our first contact, he invited me to his studio in the Jordaan. This western part of the city centre used to be the poorest; historically it was out of the main trading centre of the canal circle and grew as an industrialised, rough area. In the 20th century, the Jordaan began to regenerate and especially the old Amsterdam music culture became vibrant in the area. Now it's home to many small art galleries and *hofjes* [small garden courtyards], as well as one of the city's most sought-after housing locations.

It's also a place where a famous face can go about his business undisturbed. Def P's atelier is in Tichelstraat, a narrow and beautiful street, so typical of the Jordaan.

His small, 20 sq metre studio is covered with psychedelic and fluorescent artworks and, as I enter, I find the man behind the Def P persona busy with an oil painting.

Our Amsterdam lives have followed completely different paths. I've spent years in a suit and tie, being Mr. Canon. Pascal has been on radio, stage and TV, creating commotion with his art, and opinions, at every turn.

Yet this meeting is the beginning of a connection that will last throughout the development of this book. Born and raised in the city, Pascal embraces its concept, while adding his unique creativity.

As we start to talk, Pascal and I find we have more in common than just a passion for Amsterdam.

I've just returned last week from a world trip. I recently got married and I've always had a big wish to travel, so my wife and I decided it might be fun to have a honeymoon all around the world.

We took the train east – Germany, Poland, Belarus, Russia, Mongolia, China, Tibet, Japan – and then we flew over the ocean and across Canada. We took the broadest part of land that you can travel over eastwards, so we could experience how big the world really is.

I hand over my book about my own recent world trip as a gift and we share some stories about travelling.

We crossed country borders 10 times during the trip, and every one of those times there was thunder and lightning. That's crazy, huh? Then one night, after we'd been back in Amsterdam for a couple of days, there was a massive crash of thunder. We thought, *Okay, the Thunder God is giving us a final message to round off the trip.* There's certainly something in my life about co-incidence.

Pascal enthusiastically flicks through the book. As a new writer, I'm always impressed when somebody whose music has been regularly published treats your first work as something special. Fame has not eroded Pascal's ability to encourage those still at the beginning.

We begin to talk about his Amsterdam experiences.

Yes, I'm an *'echte Amsterdammer'* [real Amsterdammer] – born in the Wilhelmina Gasthuis, in the Kinkerbuurt. It was '69, almost the same time as Jim Morrison was in the same hospital. He came to Amsterdam for one day and swallowed a big chunk of hashish and couldn't handle it. He could have been my neighbour in the hospital. Maybe that was the inspiration for my music career!

My family moved out of the centre when I was 11 and we lived in Osdorp until I was 19. Then I lived in the east of Amsterdam with an interesting view of the Dappermarkt – and now I'm back in the centre again.

To begin with, I studied to be a printer before switching to a diploma in graphic design. That was my job from 20–25 years old, though I was always making music as a hobby. I was working 60 hours a week at my design job, for a really small salary, 1,400 guilders a month – that's 600 euros today.

When I started performing, some months I was making more money from the shows than from my job. I began to think, *I'm crazy – a couple of hours of music earns me more than working all these hours in my job.* So I switched it around and decided, *Fuck it, I'm gonna make music full-time.*

Graphic design was always a serious part of my music career, because the band needed flyers, T-shirts, logos, album covers, merchandise. I designed all that stuff, so the studying came in pretty handy.

Chatting over coffee in his atelier, I find it hard to imagine this man

IT'S A REAL PART OF THE AMSTERDAM CULTURE – DON'T PUT YOURSELF ABOVE THE OTHER

as Def P, ranting out his hard-hitting words on stage. He explains how he got started.

I was the first to rap in Dutch, and it came about when I was visiting relatives in LA back in 1988. I was 18 and fanatical about gangster rap, so being there made me feel I was in the Mecca of my music.

A few guys and I got together and were rapping in English, but it's difficult in a language that's not your own. At a certain point we were freestyling and I just started doing it in Dutch. They all reacted like, "Hey man, that's fresh! I never heard something like that." It struck me that the rappers in Europe were making it difficult for themselves by trying to do it in English.

That encouraged me to make my first real demo tape in '89. I sold it to friends and gave it away, and it got popular. Soon some friends and I had put a band together and we got a TV break in 1990 as the first Dutch rap group. Suddenly everybody knew who we were and then it just exploded; we were Osdorp Posse from Amsterdam, those four crazy little white guys rapping in Dutch.

We started touring, and – well, to cut a long story short – over the next 20 years we experienced a lot of crazy shit. All the stuff you can imagine about being in a band? We did it. It was a wild adventure and we really had a good time, but life moves on and you have to close the chapter.

To round off our career together, the band had two great sell-out farewell concerts at the Melkweg, my favourite venue to play at in Amsterdam. When we came on stage, two or three guys in the front row threw their hands up with their beers and shouted, and within a split second the whole audience had done the same – everyone wet, total chaos. It was almost like it was arranged; yet really it was spontaneous. I had goosebumps.

I wonder what it's like to be well known in Amsterdam.

Fame doesn't mean too much to Amsterdammers and there's a bit of their arrogance with that attitude. They see you and then act like they don't recognise you or didn't notice you. *Just because you're on TV doesn't mean you're better than me* is the message. It's a real part of the Amsterdam culture – don't put yourself above the other.

For a person with a famous face, that's very comfortable. I think a lot of successful people want to live here because the locals are not so enthusiastic about fame and they leave you alone.

I experience this as we wander to the bakery on the corner of Westerstraat and Tichelstraat for Pascal's favourite 'millennium sandwich' – nobody gives him a glance. We sit on the terrace of De Blauwe Pan café opposite the bakery and the waitress comes out, seemingly angry, and tells us, "It doesn't look good if you're sitting on my terrace with food that's not from me!" After a small exchange between the two of them, Pascal explains something about Amsterdam humour.

This was an example that shows how humour here is about resistance – you have something thrown at you, so you have to come back with something. It's as if they try to piss you off and see how you react. If you react in a funny way and even try to piss them off too, it's like 1-1 and then it's okay. If someone makes a joke like that, and you react by being offended, then it's 1-0 to them; it's like a little game.

Pascal really cares about his city and gives me his view on what's changed in recent years.

Amsterdam is changing, and we're are right to complain about that sometimes. All kinds of little things are happening. They want to replace the *Amsterdammertjes* [red bollards with three vertical crosses], because apparently they're too expensive to maintain. There's talk about getting rid of the herring stalls and even the flower kiosks. Everybody knows about the Red Light District windows closing one by one and more regulations for coffeeshops. But all of that stuff is typical Amsterdam! All these things are icons which give us an image as a city, and they keep fucking with them. If they go on like this, it'll be like any other metropolis, with a lot of rules and where you can't do anything.

It's still a great place and for sure, Amsterdam is one of my biggest inspirations. When I paint, there is normally something from the city influencing me; it's a stimulating place to make pictures of. You have all kinds of different styles of buildings, and there are no straight lines anywhere - that fits especially when you paint in the kind of psychedelic way that I do, with very bright colours. It's really alive, this city; I try to capture that in my paintings. Most of the time I create scenes without people, to show it's really the *city* that's alive.

Amsterdam's crooked and raggedy – that's why it's great to paint it. I make these more realistic paintings of the city too. Sometimes I don't have to exaggerate the colours because they are so bright already.

As I look around the studio, I notice Pascal uses all kinds of different artistic approaches in his art.

I haven't found my style yet. Some friends tell me I have, but it's hard for me to agree. I learned all these different types of art in my past and I don't know which one is really my own – so I'm still experimenting. I'm beginning to get more graphic, doing stuff that's simpler with fewer details and working more with lines and colour.

Luckily, through being in Osdorp Posse, I became known as a designer as well as a rapper. Many fans liked the graphic stuff I did and knew it was me who designed it – I've even seen hundreds of tattoos of my logos and designs. Maybe that's the biggest compliment you can get, someone putting your art permanently on their bodies.

People liked my lyrics which prompted magazines and websites to ask me to write different stuff. Just by being a rapper, I became a writer too, and graphic design became a more artistic thing to do. Moving onto painting was a logical development.

Later I was asked, "I'm making a theatre play, can you make some raps for me?" Then, "Can you write a whole theatre play?" Now there are opportunities to do all kinds of things, and all this from being a rapper in a band.

I like that diversity of creative work, and you can do it in Amsterdam because there are so many niches and different areas of art. I'm distracted quite easily and get bored fairly quickly, so it's lucky that I feel like a kid who is playing all day long – if I don't want to play with this, I play with something else. I only do what I like; I feel blessed that I can do it that way.

THERE'S A TYPICAL ARROGANCE THAT COMES OUT IN THE AMSTERDAM HUMOUR

Getting an insight into the background of one of Pascal's most eye-catching creations is really a privilege.

This painting's a tribute – the guy is a deformed shape of Albert Hofmann, the inventor of LSD. He died at 102 years old - amazing, huh? Even at 100 years old he was still sharp enough to lecture to scientists at conferences. When I heard he'd died, I thought I'd give him a tribute, because I had so many great times on LSD!

I made it look like he's tripping with all these mushroom elements in the background. In Dutch we say *gedachtekronkel* [twisted mind] and I created that, literally, straight up to heaven. He has an open mind too. And the background colours of the mushrooms on his shoulders are fluorescent, which means all the greens and yellows will pop out in a room with fluorescent lighting.

You'll notice my logo in the picture, a microphone ending in a pen or a paintbrush. The wings stand for the freedom to say and write what you want. That's a fundamental belief of mine, which is why I tattooed the logo onto my arms.

The essence of Amsterdam? Freedom, atmosphere, alive, choices. Great artists put on concerts, there are lots of exhibitions, museums – there's everything you want. The essence is also arrogance, because the people living here know that Amsterdam is one of the greatest places in the world to live. I think a bit of that arrogance comes out in the typical Amsterdam humour; the locals say the Netherlands is Amsterdam and the rest is grass and cows. Of course we say this to piss off the Rotterdammers...

www.defpenco.nl
www.bl3nder.nl

NIEUWE DOELENSTRAAT

Even in Amsterdam's city centre, it's possible to find calm as most travel by foot and bike rather than by car. A specialist in the city's most tranquil spots is Siobhan Wall.

A BIG FACTOR IN MOVING HERE WAS BEING ABLE TO LIVE NEAR THE CITY CENTRE WITHOUT A CAR

SIOBHAN WALL

AMSTERDAMMER SINCE 2000
AUTHOR OF 'QUIET AMSTERDAM' AND 'QUIET LONDON'
FAVOURITE AMSTERDAM LOCATION – HORTUS BOTANICUS, PLANTAGEBUURT

Some might think that 'quiet Amsterdam' is a contradiction in terms, but Siobhan Wall realised the potential of the city's secret, placid spots in her book of that title.

The loud, creative spark and decadence of Amsterdam is offset by the tranquillity of libraries, bookshops and parks. One of the beauties of Amsterdam is that you can walk across a crowded square such as Leidseplein, along with hundreds of others, and just a few hundred metres further on you can find yourself in quiet backstreets. A minute away from the main tourist track and you can wander slowly along the canals and bridges, and take in the age-old buildings.

My own favourite quiet spot is... well, I'm not sure I want to tell you, in case it doesn't stay quiet.

Siobhan brought the calmer side of Amsterdam to light in her book, and the surprise factor must surely have been a part of the concept's success. She looks at the city in a way that's different to the conventional, reputed image of Amsterdam.

I also came a little closer to the ever-elusive answer to the question: Why do creative people come to Amsterdam?

One of Amsterdam's main attractions is its many campaign organisations. For instance, I was the artist-in-residence with the *Clean Clothes Campaign*, supporting garment workers worldwide; their headquarters are in Amsterdam.

Such organisations emerged in the '80s, along with the squatter movement and the anti-Vietnam war protests. Lots of former squats became legal living locations in the '80s, and often they turned into various kinds of cultural centres. Het Fort van Sjakoo on Jodenbreestraat is a good example. It's an international bookshop with a focus on radical writings, and developed out of a former squat.

For me, those buildings and the individuals who live or work in them typify Amsterdam. The buildings have low, subsidised rent, enabling people to do what many would describe as 'alternative activities', taking the initiative to use empty buildings. That's what's unique about the city – you don't see much of that in London or elsewhere in England. I like the fact that around here there's private housing side by side with a Salvation Army hostel and some social housing. That means an area even very close to the centre of the city is extremely diverse, and that's unique to Amsterdam too.

We sit in Siobhan's apartment close to the Artis zoo, surrounded by piles of books and magazines. She is a person completely absorbed in culture and art – a passion fed by the city she's lived in for over 10 years. Siobhan also revels in the simplicity of getting around a capita; that's smaller than anyone imagines.

A big factor in moving here from England was when I learned it was possible to live near the centre of a major city without a car. Neither I nor my husband have a driving licence, so being able to reach everything on foot or by bike, yet still have some peace and greenery, made the city the perfect location for us.

Another big attraction was that there's a lot of contemporary art here, and in particular a lot of galleries. I had read that Amsterdam has, per capita, enough cultural activities for a city 50 times its size. There are only 10 days in the year when there isn't a festival on in Amsterdam! Some of my favourites are the Canal Festival *[Grachtenfestival]*, a June weekend when all the canal gardens are open, and the Holland Festival, where you get to see cutting-edge international theatre. So when I looked at Amsterdam as a place to live, I knew that on any evening I would be able to go and see contemporary dance, or listen to jazz or world music. These days I like going to the Tropentheater, because I love Turkish and Iranian music.

It is a cultured city. People will spend time browsing in bookshops and appreciating ideas, and they value whatever is currently happening in theatre, dance, art and music.

Another factor is the amazing access I have to so many libraries, all within biking distance. Libraries are crucial for researching my projects. You can buy an annual library ticket for around 40 euros that gives you access to every resource you might need in Amsterdam – from the Tropeninstituut's library, which concentrates on geographical and developmental studies, to public libraries, two university libraries and even the postgraduate art school library at the Rijksakademie.

At the moment I'm primarily writing books, and spending less time curating in exhibition spaces, but I like to think that I'm curating exhibitions in my books. I see the photographs in *Quiet Amsterdam* as a 'portable exhibition'; one that people can take around with them.

I'm lucky to have a studio in central Amsterdam. That's another reason to be here, because artists are very well supported, and there are organisations that rent out buildings waiting to be sold.

During the past months, I've met a lot of artists and wondered what it is that draws creative people to the city. Siobhan is a very analytical thinker who speaks with a measured reasoning, so I appreciate her own theory on this.

The Netherlands, as a whole, is relatively prosperous and people's lives are quite comfortable, which means they don't really want anything to disturb what's known and safe. The ones who find that a bit too conformist tend to come to Amsterdam.

As a result you get the creative, the rebellious, and the anarchistic – the kind of characters who would probably face some social censure or criticism in towns outside of Amsterdam. They find refuge here, I think.

I've come to know a lot of the artists by writing about their work. I write press releases for a small ceramics gallery called De Witte Voet, and that's a really good way to get to know others. Almost all the Dutch people I know in Amsterdam are artists who have come from outside the city; the locals tend to stick to their own circle of friends that they built up during school or university. The artists see themselves a little like outsiders within Amsterdam society, providing insights that can't be found elsewhere in our consumerist society.

That 'outsider' feeling partly exists because their work isn't appreciated as it might be in England or France. Take an artist like Wilma Bosland, who makes amazing hand-thrown ceramic pieces. She produces a kind of vase, but then squashes it into the shape of a child's dress or a skirt. It's all done by hand so you can even see her thumbprints. Her work is very powerful because it's about female bodies, not pretty landscapes. It's looking more at what's underneath everyday encounters, the unspoken. Not many see her work, however, because the observations she makes are not part of mainstream culture, and therefore she gets limited coverage.

Dutch artists I know tell me that Dutch reviewers don't value work that's produced by local artists unless it's got a very good reputation abroad. If a famous London artist comes to Amsterdam, the Dutch press will immediately write about it. However, if there's an exhibition in a small Dutch gallery, even if the work is fascinating and profound, few Dutch reviewers have the confidence to write about it unless international art critics have already validated it.

You could say that, in the Amsterdam art world, productivity is very high, but visibility very low! I was lucky because the Amsterdammers do have an interest in how foreigners see their city, so my book sold

VISITORS SHOULD GO TO THE GREEN SPACES SUCH AS AMSTELPARK, NOT JUST VONDELPARK. THERE ARE MANY BEAUTIFUL SPOTS ON THE EDGE OF THE CITY

well even though I was not an especially well-known artist at all.

It was a review in national newspaper *de Volkskrant* that sparked wide interest in Siobhan's book, *Quiet Amsterdam*. She explains how she distributed deliveries to the bookshops using the most obvious method – by bike.

The idea for *Quiet Amsterdam* was originally a practical one. I'm deaf in my left ear so I have to go to quiet restaurants, otherwise I can't participate in conversation. I've always been an explorer – since I was very young I've enjoyed going walking and cycling, and I love taking photographs. I thought it would be rewarding to put those interests together and show other people hidden places, quite unlike the familiar image of Amsterdam.

It was so pleasurable to make the book, because I'm quite adventurous and I like doing things on my own. I'd cycle off in the direction of De Poel, a lake just outside the city, and then head to Flevopark, or to the woods at Amsterdamse Bos. All were unknown to me, and being

in a foreign country and finding new parks really gave me a sense of discovery. If I like something, I want to let others know about it and I felt the best format to let others know about Amsterdam's quieter places was a book. I published a limited edition – and it proved so popular that it sold out.

My new book, *Quiet London*, was launched in April 2011 and it proved harder to do. Amsterdam's a lot more photogenic. I think everyone should discover the green spaces outside of Vondelpark, especially tourists staying for more than a couple of days; there are so many beautiful spots outside the city. Vondelpark is great and has its own character, but it's not as intriguing as Erasmuspark, the Hortus Botanicus or the Westerpark. Maybe people don't want to risk getting lost or ending up going somewhere that might be a disappointment. That's why I put photographs in the book – to show just how enticing these places are.

One woman who bought the book wrote to me, saying she's going to visit every location in it – my ideal reader! Maybe the readers like the idiosyncratic perspective. I mean, it's not the conventional tourist guide at all – it's certainly not Lonely Planet. I am glad that the readers appreciated something different.

It was my first book, so everything was very exciting; going to the printers to see it rolling off the presses, seeing a square pile of paper as tall as me – that makes you a bit nervous! I just didn't know whether it would sell or if I'd be left with piles of books in my studio.

I started out promoting it by going to the small press fair in Paradiso. Then the buyer at Waterstone's bookshop on Kalverstraat became very enthusiastic and arranged a book signing. After the *Volkskrant* review, I spent January and February cycling madly around with copies of the book in my cycle panniers to deliver all the orders. This book has been distributed by bicycle!

After many years of living here, certain things have stayed exactly the same, while others have changed significantly. For Siobhan, it's all about the bread.

When I first arrived, in 2000, restaurants were not as adventurous as they are now. But most of all for me, it's the bread shops that have changed! You could never find a bakery open on a Sunday, but now there's De Bakkerswinkel with a few branches around the city, Brood on Zeedijk, plus the Vlaamsche Broodhuys on, for example, Vijzelgracht and Elandsgracht.

Amsterdam is a city full of secrets. One other bakery, Paul Anneé in Runstraat, has sculptures made from the paper bags they put the bread in. These are simply green and white bags with orange stripes. On their own they are quite boring, but an artist makes intriguing sculptures, such as a model of the bakery itself and a complacent looking cat. That's the beautiful serendipity of living here; you go to buy bread and find delightful paper sculptures in the bakery window. For me, that is the essence of Amsterdam.

www.imagefound.com

OUDEZIJDS ACHTERBURGWAL

Hard to believe that this peaceful spot is just metres away from the famous Red Light District. Recent developments in the area include top designers showing their work side by side with the oldest business in history. And that's where I met Bas Kosters and Shirley Hart.

THERE IS A HIGH DENSITY OF CREATIVE PEOPLE IN AMSTERDAM, EVERYBODY WANTS TO BE HERE

www.myspace.com/menrbroekjevolmevrbloesjevol

BAS KOSTERS & SHIRLEY HART

BAS KOSTERS:

AMSTERDAMMER SINCE 2002

FASHION DESIGNER, MUSICIAN, DJ, TRENDSETTER

FAVOURITE AMSTERDAM LOCATION – WATERLOOPLEIN

SHIRLEY HART:

AMSTERDAMMER SINCE 1992

SINGER, STYLIST AND DJ

FAVOURITE AMSTERDAM LOCATION – THE JORDAAN

TOGETHER THEY FORM DJ DUO 'MENR. BROEKJEVOL EN MEVR. BLOESJEVOL'

I rent a desk in a grungy shared office under the train tracks leading west from the central station towards Haarlemmerplein. There are hundreds of small companies working there in units backing onto the canal, and it's a real creative mix.

The contrast with a corporate office could not be greater. Instead of fancy desks, brightly lit corridors and a clean, crisp interior, this office has concrete floors, unfinished wooden tables, posters everywhere – plus a few two-metre high portraits of naked transsexuals dotted around the place. Don't ask why. It all adds to the creative atmosphere.

Situated in this space are: a company making fitness equipment; a graphic designer; a bookkeeper; two web-developers; and three employees of Meubel Stukken, a company which organises massive Electronic Dance music parties all over the city.

One of the Meubel Stukken team is Shirley Hart, a woman who cycles to the office and does her work just like any of us there. Every now and again, she bursts into song as she goes about her business, giving a hint of her creative life.

In the weeks after I moved in, I discovered that Shirley has quite a history in Amsterdam's club scene and is part of a duo that epitomises the city's creative world. She and Bas Kosters are combining music, style and fashion wherever they go...

Bas has been part of the Redlight Fashion Amsterdam project, which enabled eighteen designers to show their work in recently emptied windows in the city's Red Light District. He and Shirley were recently voted 'Best-dressed DJs in Amsterdam' – no surprise, considering he is one of the top fashion designers in Amsterdam and she's a stylist. I went to meet them both in Bas's small flat above his atelier, in the heart of the oldest part of the city.

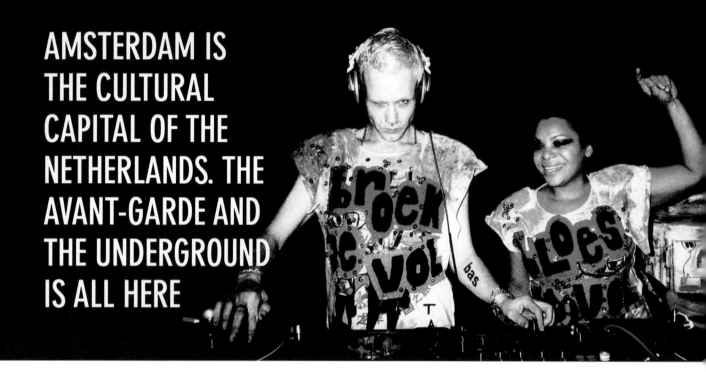

AMSTERDAM IS THE CULTURAL CAPITAL OF THE NETHERLANDS. THE AVANT-GARDE AND THE UNDERGROUND IS ALL HERE

B Shirley and I met through this mutual friend [and DJ], Jojanneke, in 2005. I decided, together with Jojanneke, to start up a party, initially called Ponchalance – a wordplay on 'party' and 'nonchalance' - to describe how we like to behave. That later developed into the Anti Fashion Party, which is where Shirley and I began DJ'ing together.

We created a name for ourselves, 'Meneer Broekjevol en Mevrouw Bloesjevol' [Mr. Trouserfull and Mrs. Blousefull] and in this way we get the chance to combine our worlds of music and fashion.

Often our bookings are fashion-related, partly because of my work and partly because of our approach. We try to give a show that looks good as well as sounds good, not like the old image of a DJ just swaying from side to side and holding an arm in the air. We're performing at places like the Amsterdam International Fashion Week, so our visual approach really fits.

I've seen Bas and Shirley performing and their DJ style is all action and colour. They look outlandish, generate energy and make a great combination.

S We get invited to perform at different kinds of parties too, because of my connection with Meubel Stukken. You know that Peter, who founded Meubel Stukken, was together with DJ Joost van Bellen in the early days of Acid House in the '90s? *[See Peter's interview on page 140.]* There are plenty of dance parties around Amsterdam and that's where we are doing sets.

Bas is also writing songs and performing in a band, and I'm a stylist working with people like Micha Klein, a very inventive computer artist. We love being in Amsterdam, working in a variety of different areas of fashion and music: most creative people here are doing more than one type of art. It's the cultural capital of the Netherlands, yet everything is so village-like because it's not too big. You can make connections with others in your field quite easily and that makes it pretty cosy – after you've been to another city, you're always glad to be back.

One tendency I've noticed amongst some older Amsterdammers is to complain that the best days of the city are gone. I mention this to Bas and ask if he feels Amsterdam has changed in the years since he first came here.

B I know a lot of Amsterdammers say the good times are over. Naturally it has changed a lot from being this hippie city in the '70s that was so liberated and so crazy, but on the other hand, I didn't experience that. This is a city I always wanted to live in and will always feel at home in. The vibe of freedom you experience here is so relaxed. Yes, perhaps I'd like to live in New York or Paris for a period of time, but I think the bond with this city will never disappear.

Amsterdam is still *the* place to be, especially if you are in fashion

or art. My brother lives in Utrecht, which is also good for music and poetry and writing, and Rotterdam is quite okay for artists too because there's a lot of space for creativity – still, I think this is the place where it's happening.

S Some designers did start up their labels in Rotterdam – like Marlies Dekkers – but after some time, they move here. Amsterdam is more relaxed and the dynamics are different than in other cities. You can be an artist in those places too – but I don't know where the secret lies in being an artist here. Is it all happening in Amsterdam, or do we just have the feeling that it's all happening here? Who knows. But there's a high density of creative people in Amsterdam; everybody wants to be here. If it's not happening here, it's just not cool, somehow.

B Here is the avant-garde, here is the underground. There's a little of that in some other places, but it just doesn't cut it, somehow – it's just a feeling. The presence of underground and diverse culture and influences in such a small city is what makes it interesting.

And you can do alternative, confrontational things here. Once I designed a fashion show of 25 minutes – normally they last around eight minutes – on a very long catwalk in the basement of the World Fashion Centre. Shirley and I sang the whole time, while 25 really great Dutch women aged 15 to 52, and from size 34 to 44, modelled the collection – such a strong, individual and diverse group. It was fabulous to challenge the norms of what models should look like and of how a fashion show should be set up. I like to add the elements of surprise and performance to my art.

I'd spoken to the creator of the Redlight Fashion Amsterdam project, Mariette Hoitink *[interview on page 44]*, just days before I met with Bas and Shirley. I am interested to know how it all came about, from an artist's perspective.

B I got called one day in January – "Bas, do you want to have an atelier and house in the Red Light District? You need to move in two weeks." I jumped at the chance! I was in a project created by the fashion recruitment agency, HTNK, called Turning Talent into Business – all of the participants got the offer. It was great timing because I really needed a place, as I had just been kicked out of my house. It came as a gift from heaven, or from the city of Amsterdam. Maybe those two are the same thing!

The project itself was quite a conversation piece, but now we're pretty well integrated into the area. It's a special project because it's so central here, whereas in other cities probably it would have been pushed to the suburbs. The presence of creatives and artists in this neighbourhood is really important.

S Central areas should represent Amsterdam's culture. The first street you see when you come from the central station is Damrak and locals call it 'the red carpet'. It needs to be appealing and diverse, a slice of what the city really is, and not just shoarma bars and coffee shops.

Are we exploited as artists to clean up the neighbourhood? We don't see it that way. Artists will always be the underdog. They will always be something untouchable. An alternative and creative presence in the neighbourhood will liven things up, and we also benefit. There are two positive sides to it.

Times certainly have changed from the '60s and '70s, when it was almost obligatory to be unusual and protest. Bas and Shirley tell me how they feel about this, considering they create some of the most outlandish looks in the city.

B Being alternative in Amsterdam is not as common these days and I do find that others stare at what I wear sometimes, but I choose not to notice because I don't *want* to be bothered. I just do and wear what I think looks good and feels good; I don't dress myself with any particular attempt to stand out or say something. The extremes of alternative culture have certainly changed, but we live in a different period now.

In the '70s, there were a lot of crazy hippies walking around here. In comparison to the establishment of that time, they were considered shocking and outspoken. There's no longer such a strong need to be really alternative from a political point of view, or to make a statement. We can express ourselves in so many ways and we have so much freedom – the freedom that those outspoken people fought for in the past.

Maybe some issues have been neglected over the years, though – for example, it's sick and stupid that we still have to protest against discrimination of homosexuals. But if the problem is there, we need to do something about it.

S It's inspiring that demonstrations have been developed by the people themselves, a Facebook community thing rather than

an organisation. There is a whole new generation who are not as tolerant. This freedom of mind, that is such a key part of Amsterdam, is not necessarily persisting, so we have to remind everyone to treasure it and honour it.

We're not stuck with the idea that a woman's place is in the kitchen – that's a good social development. So why are we still stuck with the idea that homosexuality is bad? It's important that there are people who go to schools and talk about homosexuality, who explain that it's normal and not a disease. You have to tackle discrimination at an early age; tolerance is a part of Amsterdam's history and it always should be a part of our culture.

www.myspace.com/menrbroekjevolmevrbloesjevol

THE PROJECT IS SPECIAL BECAUSE IT'S SO CENTRAL. THE PRESENCE OF CREATIVES AND ARTISTS IN THIS NEIGHBOURHOOD IS REALLY IMPORTANT

This busy square straddles the widest bridge in the city. Take a walk from here towards Central Station along Rokin, and at no. 42 you'll find the extraordinary shoes of Jan Jansen.

THE BIKE HAS INFLUENCED AMSTERDAM FASHION. YOU MUST BE ABLE TO CYCLE ACROSS THE CITY ON YOUR BIKE WITH THE CLOTHING AND SHOES YOU CHOOSE

JAN JANSEN

AMSTERDAMMER SINCE 1963
CREATOR OF OVER 2,000 SHOE DESIGNS
FAVOURITE AMSTERDAM LOCATION — ON THE CANALS, EARLY MORNING

Like so many Amsterdammers, Jan was born elsewhere – in fact, he grew up in Nijmegen. Yet having lived here for around 50 years, he more than qualifies as someone who can talk about the city's essence.

Jan immediately warmed to being a part of the book. His only stipulation was, "We should meet in the afternoon. It's more *gezellig* that way..."

If you are going to spend any time in Holland, the single word you must learn is *gezellig*. Locals will proudly tell you how difficult it is to translate the real sense of the word because it is as much about a feeling as it is about surroundings. The nearest English equivalents are either the limited 'cosy' or the out-of-date 'convivial'. A more wordy attempt to capture its meaning is: 'a combination of cosy, atmospheric, small-scale, intimate, and being among friendly people'. Jan's very specific request suggests something about him as a person.

After seeing Jan's work online, it became clear to me that he is more than a shoemaker. Rather, he is an artist using the medium of footwear. Surely these outlandish creations would be the work of an outlandish character?

And yet, as I would find so often in the coming interviews, his character is completely down-to-earth and very much grounded in the values of the city he loves.

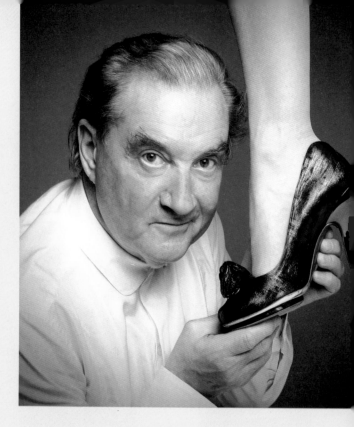

Living in Nijmegen in the late '50s was difficult if you were a little different in the way you dressed or behaved. I knew I didn't want to stay there, but wasn't sure where to go – London, Paris and Amsterdam were my 'big dream' cities. I'd already been to London and Paris many times, but on coming to Amsterdam for the first time, I knew within 10 minutes that I would stay here.

Sitting on Dam Square while eating my sandwich, I noticed that nobody was looking at me. In Nijmegen, everyone looked at me, because I always had too long hair, too tight pants or too kinky socks. I came here and found other guys and girls like me – that's why I decided to stay.

We meet in Jan's narrow office on the second floor of his shop, where so many of his ideas have started.

My life has been shoemaking, and to be honest I don't really know anything else.

I studied a few weeks at the academy in Eindhoven, where I learned how to make the paper patterns for shoes and made some of my first designs. But then I was told to change my designs and do it all in a more conventional way – I didn't like that at all! So I decided I would learn how to do it myself and took up an opportunity to be a trainee in Rome. I learned how to make shoes by hand, and with that experience behind me, came to Amsterdam in 1963.

My first workshop was in a small street called Jonge Roelensteeg, a narrow alley between two larger streets, Nieuwezijds Voorburgwal and Rokin. There was a jewelry shop there and my sister bought merchandise from the owner for her shop in Apeldoorn. She suggested I ask him for a place as a workshop and he offered me the space above his store.

It was so tiny, maybe two to three metres squared. Somebody once said to me that it looked like a big toilet! I started my work in that place and even slept there. There was no bathroom and only cold water in the shop, so I showered at the houses of friends. At the weekends I went home to Nijmegen.

The first shop opened in 1968 at Runstraat, one of *de negen straatjes* [literally, 'the nine small streets']. It's a really popular shopping area now, but at that time there was nothing but a fishmonger and a few apartments. Friends told me, "You can't open your shop in that street, nobody goes there; it's a big, big mistake." And yet, I did and stayed until 1971, when I moved to my shop here on Rokin – we've been here ever since.

In the subsequent years, Jan has gained a reputation in major shoemaking countries – and especially in Italy. I ask if he ever considered leaving for warmer climes.

I never thought of leaving Amsterdam. I do travel a lot – my wife and I had a house in Italy for 10 years, where I would stay for three

or four weeks a year – also I've worked in Italy on and off since the '70s; you could say my education and even my mentality are half Italian. But I remain an Amsterdammer, and there's no other choice – I live here and I want to die here.

In Italy, you have to wear what's fashionable this year. One year it's small python bags, the next it's big crocodile bags and everybody must have one. You don't do that in Amsterdam. You can buy an expensive brand-name jacket and wear it with second-hand trousers, and nobody cares. Everything is a mix and a melting pot here.

Amsterdam was quite a wild place when I first arrived and I felt completely free. Everything was possible in the '60s. It makes sense that the main image of that time is of the drugs culture, all the smoking and the LSD; the drugs scene was a part of the Amsterdam culture for sure, but that wasn't why I came here. I just loved the freedom, especially in the way people dressed. I still like that about living here.

No, I was never a drug person – more of a wine drinker.

I nod in agreement. "Would you like a glass of wine?" he responds. Before I have a chance to reply, he scoots upstairs and returns with a big smile and a chilled bottle of Pinot Grigio. Now it's clear why it would be more *gezellig* to meet in the afternoon...

I was once visited by a group of American tourists and we took them on a boat tour. Halfway through, one elderly gentleman said,

"This is so incredibly beautiful. Such attractive buildings and canals, and it's lovely to see all those bikes everywhere. Can I ask you – what time does it close?" They saw it as if it was a fun park! If you live here so many years, you don't see that any more. I love going to Italy, but I love coming back so that I can see the city through a visitor's eyes again.

Sometimes you're not aware of what you are experiencing. We have two sons – one is an architect, the other a philosopher. The philosopher always says to me, "You are such a lucky guy to have lived in Amsterdam during the '60s." But we didn't realise it at the time; we were just living. I do remember some things though, that were so completely different from now. For example, we lived in the Jordaan, in the west of the city centre, and we used to go by car for the short journey to Leidseplein. There were so few cars in the centre that you could drive easily and park where you liked for nothing. That's unthinkable today; driving that trip would take you longer than walking!

What is the essence of Amsterdam? A friend of mine from New York called it a *gezellige boerderij*, a cosy little farm. It's a large town with the reputation of being a big world city. No matter where I go in the world, if I say to someone, "I live in Amsterdam," they always have a look of wonder in their eyes – "Amsterdam, wow..." In some way their impression is based on the story of the coffee shops and the Red Light District. I have an assistant in Italy who's always amazed that we

don't see how unusual this city really is. He goes back to his friends and says, "There is a church in Amsterdam, and the hookers are in windows right next to it – can you believe it?" I've never thought of that as an issue, but outsiders can see it as completely crazy.

Jan's designs are unique in that his shoes are works of art. This has resulted in numerous museum exhibitions of his work.

I like that you can't see whether my shoes were designed last year, or in 1976, or in 1992. I feel I'm not creating fashion; it's rather more like industrial design. I'm not fond of the fact that patterns and colours can be considered 'in' this season, and viewed as old and worn-out six months later. 'Fashion' is in and out very quickly; my aim is to create timeless design.

Living in Amsterdam has certainly influenced my designs. If I had been a designer in Rome, I would never have made such styles, simply because I would not have had the freedom to express myself this way. See the design here with holes cut out, extra shapes and special elements? I have complete freedom to do this here, because nobody asks why I chose to make it like that. And that's good, because I don't know! There are so many things I've done in my life that I could never explain. You don't have to in Amsterdam.

The international image of Dutch fashion is on a definite upwards spiral...

Back in 1999, there was a book published on 100 individuals who have

IN ITALY, YOU HAVE TO WEAR WHAT'S FASHIONABLE THIS YEAR. HERE, YOU CAN WEAR AN EXCLUSIVE JACKET WITH SECOND HAND TROUSERS, AND NOBODY CARES

influenced Amsterdam, and I'm the only fashion person in there. If there was a similar book made now, there would definitely be more characters from a fashion or design background. Bas Kosters would be in it, as would Marlies Dekkers and Marcel Wanders. Especially in the '60s, I was always in the newspapers because there was nobody else. *'In het land der blinden is eenoog koning!'* ['In the land of the blind, the one-eyed man is king!']. I've been a teacher at the Arnhem academy and seen a whole new generation come through, but for 20 years, I was the only shoe designer in Holland.

It was much easier then, in some ways. Today they study marketing reports and look on the Internet to see what's going on. I just had a pencil, my dreams of what I wanted to create, and a great city to do it in... And a room the size of a toilet!

As I look around, I see lots of hand-drawn scraps on the table and design sheets on the walls.

Much of my design work is done here, on days when the shop is closed. I still use a piece of paper and a pencil. Design on a computer? No chance! I've done this for 50 years on my own, without assistants or trainees. I was born into this industry, as my father was a sales manager in a children's shoe factory.

Jan refills my wine glass, takes hold of a sculpted wooden mould and shows it to me as something precious and almost sacred.

For me, making shoes is like shaping masks. I shape this with my file and make these moulds all by hand. This is sculpture. Up until recently, everything was made by me.

Now there is a group of investors that want to make my sales more international. I have to train another designer, a girl that I chose, and I will teach her how to design in my style. Those investors want to continue the brand under my name. How do I feel about it? I don't know! I've had offers many times before, but they always wanted to influence my work. For example, they would say, "Okay, you designed this, but we want you to take this heart shape out because it costs money." I refused.

My contract now states that I decide 100% how the collection will be. The new designer has to follow me for the next seasons – as long as I live. [He says this with a smile and clearly plans to live a long life.]

If a client wants to buy my shoes and they want different colours, then it's okay. If they want this blue piece in red, I'm happy to do that. But the design and the lines of the shoe remain. The sculptural aspect is very important for me, because I am interested in the shape and how the different parts fit together. That is much more important to me than the colours.

We ponder the question of our city's style and Jan shows me a pair of dramatic, shiny red knee-length boots with what appear to be suede wings on the side.

This is certainly not Dutch or Amsterdam design! No, this was created specifically for Moscow Fashion Week. Dutch fashion is much less extravagant. We ask, "Can you ride to your appointment with these shoes?" The essence of Dutch fashion is functional – you have to be able to cross the city on your bike in the clothing and shoes you choose.

In London they walk to parties late at night without a coat, with uncovered arms and high heels. In the Netherlands, the number who do this is limited. We want casual, easy-going. You could even say that the bicycle has influenced Amsterdam fashion!

My final question is about Jan's more famous clients. He drinks the last of the wine and smiles...

David, this has been a very good talk, but that is a question I can't answer – it's a secret. You'll just have to write something like, "Jan Jansen keeps a tight lid on the famous names wearing his shoes."

www.janjansenshoes.com

THE RED LIGHT DISTRICT

Amsterdam's most famous area as you've never seen it. Just around the corner from
the Oude Kerk you'll find the Prostitution Information Centre, run by Mariska Majoor.

MOST PEOPLE DON'T REALISE THE RED LIGHT DISTRICT SIMPLY IS AMSTERDAM. IF YOU TAKE THAT AWAY, THEN IT'S NOT AMSTERDAM ANY MORE

MARISKA MAJOOR

AMSTERDAMMER SINCE 1985
FORMER SEX WORKER
FAVOURITE AMSTERDAM LOCATION – RED LIGHT DISTRICT

While searching for its essence, I've tried to go beyond the renowned clichés of Amsterdam. Yet a book about the city is not complete without including something about the Red Light District [RLD].

Its streets, collectively called De Wallen, have undergone a few changes in recent years, with the closing of around one third of windows being the most significant. Ventures such as the Redlight Fashion Amsterdam project have given rise to the belief that the area is on the verge of closure, to be replaced by a chic 'Armani/Dolce & Gabbana land'. Other misconceptions include the belief that all women working there are victims of human trafficking, and that the area is run entirely by drug barons and criminals.

So what better way to get past the myths than to talk to someone who has worked as a prostitute there?

Mariska Majoor formed the Prostitution Information Centre [PIC] in 1993 and has since educated thousands on the real story behind the RLD. Mariska is uniquely equipped to tell that story – she worked behind the windows for five years and is probably the most knowledgeable person about the area in Amsterdam. She speaks with a clarity that overcomes all embarrassment around a subject most find hard to broach – being a sex worker.

When we meet in De Bakkerswinkel, a bakery on Warmoesstraat around the corner from the PIC office, Mariska apologises for having limited time on this occasion to chat. "Besides, if you really want to understand prostitution, you can come another time and sit in a window for an evening. Then you will see the worker's side of the story for yourself."

Terribly sorry, I thought, *but I'm an Englishman – and you want me to sit in a prostitute window?*
I assumed she was joking, but as I got to know her better, I learned that Mariska rarely jokes about things close to her heart. And she certainly cares about ensuring the RLD is represented properly – as the oldest business district in town.

Many assume the RLD was created for the tourist industry; they often don't realise that it's the oldest part of Amsterdam, over 800 years old. In those days, this was just a tiny harbour town and, naturally, every port has to deal with horny sailors.

The history of Amsterdam's reputation is really interesting. Even in the Middle Ages, the city was well known for the tolerant way things were organised here. Amsterdam has always been what we call *onzedelijk* – how to translate that? *Zedelijk* is when you have good manners, especially towards sexual matters, and the opposite is *onzedelijk*. There have always been dancing houses and bars where sex workers picked up guys; the city was renowned for that even hundreds of years ago.

I explain to tourists that this is how Amsterdam started: you had the old church, around which they started to build a village, and bars automatically sprang up around the harbour. It all developed together to become what it is today.

These days, the authorities want to make a lot of changes and supposedly 'clean the area up'; some even imagine they will close it. But the RLD *is* Amsterdam. If you wipe prostitution out then it's not Amsterdam any more.

There's a noticeable serenity to the way Mariska communicates. She has developed into a strong and unashamed spokesperson for the sex workers in the area.

You know that in the US, they think the RLD is already closed? That's horrible! It's bad for business – bad for the girls, the hotels and restaurants, and for the local residents. The past two years were tough for all of us. I've been running the PIC for 17 years now, so I take it really personally when I hear negative talk about this area or sex work, and especially when someone talks down the workers, because they are just trying to make a living.

Whatever the plans for change, it should be respected that this is the heart of the city. Tourists are surprised when I explain that many locals live here, sometimes throughout their lives. The locals aren't against window prostitution. If the government makes plans for change – and some things do need to be changed – then they have to work together with the individuals in these streets.

We should be proud of the way the sex industry developed, in a very typical Amsterdam manner. We're very good at organising complicated social issues, not just in the sex industry, but also in relation to soft drugs, abortion, euthanasia and same-sex marriage. Outsiders imagine we teach our kids that sex is a suitable profession, or that it's good to take drugs, just because these things are legal and because we are so tolerant of the windows. Of course that's not the case; we just accept that these issues are a part of real life and not something to be hidden away.

In the past few years, the city authorities have contended there is high level of criminality in the area, claiming that's why they close down the windows. Mariska bristles at those accusations.

I really do believe it's an excuse. Let me tell you, I know the criminals around here and they are pretty harmless! The problem is that most see prostitution automatically as a bad thing. I have done presentations about sex work for many years, and it's never been as difficult as it is now to make people aware that the majority of sex workers are working of their own free will. There is so much information about trafficking being spread in the media, in the political world, in society in general. Okay, it's good that there's concern about this possible risk; there should be. I'm not saying the girls are all happy and problem free, but they are doing it out of choice, not because they are forced to.

We can't say that trafficking doesn't happen; it's a horrible thing and a major world problem, but it's not true, and unfair to pretend, that all the girls here are victims and all the owners of the establishments, criminals. The media is presenting this out of proportion.

Safety is a major reason why girls work legally here and not illegally elsewhere. They can refuse a customer, they can go to the police if they are in trouble. All rooms have very loud alarms. The girls don't have to work in dangerous circumstances on the street; they don't have to step into a car with someone they don't know and deal with the possible consequences.

Rule-makers who mix up prostitution and human trafficking could even aggravate the problem. The more windows they close, the more likely there will be some back-rooms on the edge of the city where girls have no rights or security. Instead, the authorities should focus on improving circumstances for the workers, as it is a legal profession. At the same time, they should also combat trafficking, but they shouldn't confuse the two issues.

You don't save trafficking victims by simply closing down windows.

We move to Mariska's shop, Rood, a bit further along the Warmoesstraat. Rood means red – and everything in the shop is, well, red. Her analysis and intelligence are impressive, considering she left school at 14. She smiles as she talks about her "first project as an independent woman" – the establishment of the Prostitution Information Centre.

After I quit working as a prostitute, I wanted to do something in the area and be connected to the people here. So I started a little magazine called *The Pleasure Guide* – I still produce it once in a while. I discovered that I really like working for myself and creating things relevant to sex work. Increasingly, I felt the drive to make others understand. Something like that just develops in Amsterdam, you know. I had been thinking about opening a shop, and then this place became available and from there the idea turned into reality very quickly. I started the PIC just as I had begun to work as a prostitute – impulsively. It wasn't carefully thought out; in Amsterdam you can do things that way.

I started my shop Rood in the same way a couple of years ago. I wanted to do something different from the info centre, because at the time I was really fed up with what was happening around

WE SHOULD BE
PROUD OF THE
WAY OUR SEX
INDUSTRY
DEVELOPED.
AMSTERDAM IS
VERY GOOD AT
ORGANISING
COMPLICATED
SOCIAL ISSUES

prostitution. I saw this location was for rent and, as I had the idea for the shop already, I just did it.

Many around here are like me. We are from the streets and can handle things as long as they happen out in the open. But if they happen behind desks and behind closed doors – well, that's not our style, we don't trust those kinds of methods.

Some only think about economics, while many RLD-locals think solely about the RLD. I'm trying to consider both sides, but naturally I lean towards supporting the RLD. I'm not really good at thinking at the same level as Job Cohen *[see his interview on page 126]*, because I'm not a politician. Cohen is on a level higher than most when it comes to understanding how society really works. He's open-minded and can see things from different points of view ,yet remain realistic. I find that a rare quality in politicians and city councillors.

Those desk workers make decisions that affect people on the streets. Sometimes I have to explain sex work to policy-makers who have never set foot in the RLD, who won't visit a brothel with me so I can explain more about it. They're the type who rely only on 'research', so there's a limit to what I can do. That's not the real world of the RLD.

With this thought fresh in the air, Mariska confirms her intention to put me behind a window. I agree to it – partly out of curiosity and partly because it would have seemed uninformed of me not to. The following Saturday I find myself sitting on a stool, a shady figure in the PIC window that's decorated as a traditional hooker's bedroom. Mariska seems to enjoy my discomfort, and while we watch the faces of the passers-by change from embarrassed interest to bemusement, she tells me about her first impressions from behind the window.

I was born in Hilversum and came to work and live in Amsterdam when I was 17; I'd already worked as a prostitute in Hilversum for a while, but this was very different. My first impressions of Amsterdam? Being so young, everything looked big and exciting. The city's like a village to me now, but when I first arrived and started going to discos and doing a little drugs, I was captured by the atmosphere of freedom.

My first working experiences in Amsterdam, in the summer of 1984, brought a quick transformation. On the first night, I was too scared to stand up and kept the curtains half-closed. It was busy, crowded, exciting, but also a little scary, strange and wild. Within a couple of days, I became part of that scary thing myself, and it surprised me how quickly I got used to it. It was actually a lot of fun and really exciting, even though it was quite a strange period of my life. I made a lot of friends here, also in the criminal corner of life.

People find that hard to accept, because they have certain images about criminals, but there are different levels of criminality. A certain level of illegality is common around here, but nothing like what is happening in other parts of the city or in other parts of the country. Police presence in the RLD is very high, and there are strong social controls too because we look out for each other.

It's tougher now for the prostitutes than it was in my day, especially because rent for the rooms has risen faster than the prices they can charge. For example, a girl may need five customers before the rent is covered for a twelve-hour shift. That fifth customer may not arrive until the tenth or eleventh hour, which then leaves just an hour or so to earn money for herself.

Earlier that evening, I'd heard Mariska doing one of her many tours for tourists. A wave of shock rippled through the audience when she casually explained the requirements for being a prostitute: "No qualifications needed – you don't need a diploma in blowjobs."

Some of the questions I get are funny. Sometimes they ask, "How does it work? If a guy wants to go to a prostitute, what questions does he ask?" I say, "No big deal. He goes to the window and asks how much", but they can't imagine it can be that simple.

"Does she know what he means?" "Well, it's pretty clear," I tell them. "The girl will ask, 'Do you want a blow job, do you want straight sex, what kind of position do you want, do you want to play a game?'" The tourists from more conservative countries are always shocked at how straightforward it all is.

I like sitting here in the window so much. You get a really different view on a person from in here. When you're walking on the street, it's hard to focus and it's a different kind of contact. From the window you can see inside them. You can identify the different aspects of their character, how they really are - depressed, happy, honest. If someone is aggressive, I can't see it on the street, but from here, I know it immediately. To observe a person's reaction when they see a window prostitute is like removing a mask.

Some say you should be careful with what kind of customers you take in, but the girls know everything. From here, you can look a potential client in the eyes and see from their body language whether you can trust them or not, how they might be as a customer, what they will be willing to pay.

You see how some are afraid to look at us? It's interesting that they are too embarrassed to look - even though they've made the decision to come to the windows!

She is direct about a subject most prefer to avoid, though she understands why they might want to.

It's too hard for most to talk about their emotions; they always project onto others. I try not to do that. I think you should never be embarrassed about something you've done, unless it caused harm. I don't take a moral standpoint because I don't care what you do, as long as you don't hurt anyone. There is nothing wrong with being a prostitute, if it's your choice. There is everything wrong if you're forced to be a prostitute.

People might think being a prostitute is something to be embarrassed about, but they are probably talking about their own feelings towards sex work. I can't say it was easy, but it was very interesting and I learned a lot. I didn't always feel comfortable at the time, but I feel comfortable looking back and don't have any regrets.

If I had to choose between being proud or embarrassed, I'd certainly choose to be proud.

www.pic-amsterdam.com

www.roodismooi.nl

DE MAGERE BRUG

Translated by the tourist boat commentary as 'The skinny bridge'. This busy and beautiful crossing over the Amstel river is just a few steps away from Carré, a theatre which Youp van 't Hek regularly makes his own.

YOU HAVE TO BE A LITTLE CRAZY TO BE AN ARTIST, AND AMSTERDAM IS THE PLACE TO DO IT

YOUP VAN 'T HEK

AMSTERDAMMER SINCE 1973
COMEDIAN, AUTHOR, SINGER
FAVOURITE AMSTERDAM LOCATION – CARRÉ THEATRE

Being a comedian in Holland and working in Dutch naturally limits your market. Outside of Holland, only some Belgians will understand the language, which is similar to – but, careful, not the same as – the Flemish spoken by a few million.

Youp van 't Hek is a man who stretches those limits as far as possible. He's best known as a comic, and he tours his shows relentlessly across the country for months on end, while regularly appearing on TV to comment on current issues. He has released numerous musical and comedy records throughout his career, published a number of books, and writes a hugely popular weekly column in the *NRC* newspaper – Holland's highest quality daily. Those columns are converted into a book every year, and over four million of these have been sold.

And it doesn't stop there. As he arrives for our talk, Youp apologises for being a little late, explaining he had been to see his grandson with the first print of his latest children's book, *Sinterklaas en het kleine hoogtevreespietje* [Saint Nicholas and his little helper with vertigo]. "I promised to bring him that copy personally and read it to him – well, he's only 16 months, so I guess he didn't understand much! But I wanted to keep the promise."

Youp launches into stories about his early experiences of Amsterdam in fluent English, and slips into Dutch only when talking about football.

My first Amsterdam jobs were in offices. You see all those companies on the Frederiksplein there? I worked for most of them for a few weeks. It was good for me, because it motivated me to make a success out of my performing career – if I didn't succeed, I would have to go back to an office job.

After I arrived in Amsterdam in 1973, I stayed in a tiny room for 35 guilders [15 euros] a month. I wrote my first poems and jokes there, while I searched for small theatres and podiums to play at. With my tiny salary, I rented a small theatre of about 80 seats. Sometimes three people would come to my performance, sometimes five. I didn't care, because I was still a student having fun, drinking, telling jokes. Amsterdam was a really free place then, and from the moment I arrived, I loved it. There was such a reaction to the small-thinking 1950s, and when the pill and the drugs came in the '60s, the place completely opened up. I was enjoying it all! I had no money, but it was fun.

I kept doing my show and trying to improve – and gradually the audience increased to 20, then 40, and finally I got booked for a tour in 1984. That's when it really took off, but it had taken time and a lot of work to get there. Before that tour, I played at events for companies and small football clubs, where the audience would be drunk before you even set foot onstage. They'd shout at you, thinking they were so funny; that's when you learn how to handle those kinds of characters in an audience.

Of course I hoped my performing career would be a success, but I never imagined I'd end up playing the Carré theatre for weeks!

I'd seen Youp cycling along the street across the canal from Café Marcella, where we were due to meet. His head and hair are incredibly distinctive – you know it's him in an instant. As a man who makes his living out of talking, it's not difficult to get him going when I mention having read that, behind his sometimes harsh and sarcastic act, he is an idealist.

Yes, I am an idealist and I believe in a lot of things – that's the heart of my comedy. Most of all, I believe we have to realise we have a good life, and we should live it. When I hear about people taking antidepressants and so on, I say, "Come on! We are a rich country, we live in a great city – dream, live, be! If things are going wrong, then take it on, change it! Don't wait around, but live your life."

What I like about Amsterdam is that you can live in your own way, even if you're odd or different. That's difficult in villages or small towns, but here it's possible. I like those those who are a bit odd or being unconventional. You have to be a little crazy to create something and be an artist – and Amsterdam is the place to do it.

You can expect that some will dislike you for it, and that's okay. It's better to get a negative reaction than none at all. If you tell your friends that you're going to my show, some are going to say, "Great, you'll love it" and others will say, "Forget it, he's terrible." And that's fine with me! I don't sit in the middle about anything; I say what I think. If someone doesn't like it, no problem.

My father was real Amsterdam. He and his brothers used to tell jokes about everything. They never believed politicians or the news, and were always contrary and questioning. That's the essence of Amsterdam humour, the real humour of the old city is all about being opposite to something. It makes you unpopular at times, but you have to live with that if you want to remain authentic.

One of Youp's best known columns is called *Pretpark Amsterdam* – describing the city as an amusement park, with endless possibilities for the city-dwellers to entertain themselves. His own city pursuits are quite modest.

My favourite things of Amsterdam are pretty simple – just being around town, drinking coffee in an old café, riding along the canals on my bicycle, going to a museum. I visit the Concertgebouw at least once a month because I love classical music – the quality of shows and acoustics there is as good as anywhere in the world. We should be proud of the many impressive qualities of our city. I really hope Amsterdammers understand the importance of the UNESCO World Heritage listing of our canal circle, the *grachtengordel*. It's more difficult to enjoy being on the water now, because in the past ten years, the number of drunk tourist parties on boats has increased. But sometimes I take my boat out to cruise around at

THE REAL HUMOUR OF OLD AMSTERDAM IS ALL ABOUT BEING OPPOSITE TO SOMETHING

5 am and that's when Amsterdam is so beautiful, riding along the Prinsengracht to the Brouwersgracht and onto the River IJ. Nobody around, very calm. Especially early on a Sunday morning – it's as if the rest of the city is still sleeping off its hangover.

That's why I raised my son and my daughter here, because I love it so much and I wanted them to have this Amsterdam experience too. If I'm playing shows in Rotterdam, afterwards I might call my daughter and she'll say, "We're in this café, come and join us." I'll arrive late in the evening at a small place on a corner, low light, friends talking and drinking – that's the real *gezelligheid* of Amsterdam, the cosy feeling that I look forward to so much.

After I had initially moved to Amsterdam, I did leave once – to live with a girlfriend who had a job and apartment in the south-west of the Netherlands. Unfortunately, I only lasted a single day. On the first evening, I went to a small shop nearby our apartment and picked up a bottle of wine. At the counter, the owner said, "Your girlfriend bought the same bottle yesterday." I looked at him and thought, *Great, I'm here for just one day, and he knows what kind of wine we drank last night.* My partner came home that night and I told her, "We're leaving tomorrow!"

You can be pretty anonymous in Amsterdam, even if you're well known, but I tend to avoid the bars late at night because people are drunk and become brave – "Hey, there's Youp!" One guy comes up to tell you "You're the best"; the next says, "You're ugly"; another shouts across the bar, "Your last column was terrible!" and so on. Sometimes they stand there and say, "I know a guy, he went to the same school as you." What do you say in reply? Well done? I just say, "Thanks. Now I'll talk to the girl I came here with, okay?"

They don't want to talk to you as a person; they want Youp, the character on stage. But after the show, I'm a typical guy who wants to talk about football, women, beer, politics – not about me. During the day, when they're sober, it's not a problem because they can talk about those things like normal people.

Another of my favourite things about Amsterdam is going to watch Ajax football club. I've been a fan for 38 years.

I don't know why, but for a moment I think I'm a funny guy too and make a joke along the lines of, "So you're a masochist?" He looks at me blankly. "Supporting Ajax? You like to cause yourself pain?" He ignores the joke and moves on.

Every year my brother and I say, "Come on, this was terrible. We'll never go again!" And then, of course, we go again, because we always have the hope that, one day, we'll find someone like Cruijff. He's my favourite Ajax player of all time, Johan.

My father liked Piet Keizer, but for me it was always Johan. He came into the team when I was just 10 years old and the city called him Jopie. He was a hero, a real hero.

At my fiftieth birthday, my friends arranged a wonderful surprise party for me, and Jopie sent a video message. Typical Cruijff, you know, he's well known for these sayings that leave you wondering if they mean something or nothing. He began by saying, *"Nou ja, omdat ik niet bij u ben, zit ik hier."* ["Well, because I'm not there with you, I'm sitting here."] And he ended the speech by saying, *"Nou, hebben ze het toch goed bekeken. Iedereen voor lul zetten, en daarmee je zakken vullen."* ["Good job, Youp – there you go, making fun of everybody, and filling your pockets from it."]

We had a few good players in the past, but it's been a while now. The twins were good, Ronald and Frank de Boer. We had Dennis Bergkamp for a couple of years, and Danny Blind was a good leader, but we can only dream of the kind of team Ajax had in the '70s – an absolute dream team, with Sjakie Swart *[see the interview on page 104]*, Jopie, Neeskens.

Controversy is part of a comedian's life, and Youp has never been afraid to court it by speaking his mind. Yet there is one subject that he avoids these days – football hooligans. A column in the *NRC* on that subject caused him the most trouble.

Louis van Gaal [former coach of Ajax and the Dutch national team] became a friend of mine. When his wife was dying, he asked her, "What would make you happy?" She answered, "I've never been to a Youp van 't Hek show." They came and we met backstage afterwards – such a nice couple - and that was how we became friends. Sadly she died soon after.

Ajax played Rotterdam club Feyenoord a few weeks later, and before the game there was a lot of concern about the abuse the fans used to shout at each other. The authorities threatened to stop the game if the fans chanted things that were too extreme. During the match, the Feyenoord fans started singing terrible things – "Louis van Gaal, he lives alone" and *"Hij had een kankerwijf"* [He had a cancer-wife]. Nobody should have to hear those things while grieving – nobody. You have to respect your fellow human being.

The following Saturday, I wrote in my *NRC* column, "They told us that when the abuse is too extreme, they'll stop the game. So was this not too much? When do you stop the match? When is it too much?" I asked the mayor and the head of the police. I pushed this point as far as I could, because I really thought the chants were extreme and that they should answer the question. The subject was even raised in parliament.

After the column was published, some police who had infiltrated the Feyenoord hooligans told the Amsterdam police, "If Youp plays in Rotterdam, it's not safe for him. They plan to get him." Well, I wanted to go ahead with the shows anyway – I didn't want to be bullied – but I had bodyguards for two quite some time. Nobody knew about it and it was never in the press, but everywhere I went, there were two guys with me. If I had to pee, they were right there next to me.

One of my friends said, "When I heard what you said, I thought, 'Okay Youp, you are right – but don't write it in the newspaper! You're asking for trouble.'" I don't regret writing it, but I love my wife, I love my children, I love my grandson, I love my life. I will not die for that. I will die for a lot of things, but not that.

I've never really understood that kind of violence; I hate fighting. I like talking, joking, I like discussing with everybody. The best weapon is words, because people can listen or switch off.

I remind Youp of the Buckler beer story, which also enveloped him in controversy.

Yeah, that was big, I suppose. Heineken was about to introduce a new alcohol-free beer, called Buckler, in the Netherlands. Every year on 31 December I do the *oudejaarsconference* [New Year's Eve show] and I decided to make jokes about the kind of man who would drink it. You could say it was harsh, but my issue wasn't with the brewery; I just don't like people saying something is what it's not. Making an alcohol-free beer is like selling meat-free sausages, and I made some fun of the kind of guy who might drink Buckler. It was just part of a joke-set, nothing personal.

The whole launch failed as a result. It was already selling in France, and they expected millions of bottles to go in Holland. I made that beer – well, I made it stop. It was a bit merciless, but I don't regret it. Some years later, a couple of guys from Heineken came to me after a show and they just laughed about it.

Recently, I launched a magazine called *De Help,* because I'd had some bad experiences with the T-Mobile help desk. I asked the public to send me their own stories and suddenly we had a whole magazine! Those big companies need shaking up sometimes.

His renowned hard edge had been almost invisible in our talk. I hear the same thing from all friends and fans of his – Youp can be cynical in his comedy, but is incredibly loyal and supportive to those around him. At the end of our meeting, he invites me to his show at Carré, and backstage I meet a number of people who have been working with him for over 20 years.

Youp's well known for having the last word, and I thought it would be fitting if he wrote a piece for the book as an 'afterword', in contrast to a foreword. He simply has to make a joke about this.

The best last words I ever heard were from a friend of mine. He knew he was dying and when he thought it was nearly time, he asked his wife to lean forward. He whispered in her ear, "In a few moments, I'll know."

www.youp.nl

WESTERGASFABRIEK

Formerly a gasworks, it was converted into one of the coolest and most atmospheric places for Amsterdammers to enjoy concerts, movies and art. Mark de Kruijk is the cultural centre's director.

CYCLISTS ARE THE MODERN ANARCHISTS OF AMSTERDAM

MARK DE KRUIJK

AMSTERDAMMER SINCE 1976
DIRECTOR OF WESTERGASFABRIEK CULTURE PARK
FAVOURITE AMSTERDAM LOCATION – VONDELPARK

Amsterdam has the ambition to be an attractive city on a global level for both business and tourists. Balancing the needs to preserve its ancient centre and continually modernise its cultural and economic attractions is no easy task.

Money that came from the economic success of the '90s has been invested into major development projects, such as the renovation of both the Rijksmuseum and the Stedelijk Museum, and a new metro line running through the very centre of the city. Meanwhile, the business district in the south has a long-term plan to grow massively. This constant improvement has helped Amsterdam to be consistently rated in the top five cities in the world, based on commercial criteria as well as measures of quality of life.

Mark de Kruijk is well placed to comment on these various challenges facing the city's future. He headed up a city development project called Amsterdam Topstad [Top City] for five years, following on from a number of positions involved in city communications. Now he's Director of one of the most thriving cultural hotspots in Amsterdam.

In 1981, I remember there was a huge demonstration in Amsterdam, involving a crowd of 400,000 marching against nuclear weapons. I was only 16 and living in the quieter northern area of the country, near Groningen. When I heard about this event, I simply had to be part of it. The energy of the protest and the city both completely captured me and I decided to move here as soon as possible. That was over 25 years ago, so by now I consider myself an Amsterdammer. It's something I am proud of, so much so that when my wife was about to give birth, we went to a hospital in the centre instead of one on the outskirts, just to be sure my daughter would also be able to say, "I am an Amsterdammer!"

Mark brims with enthusiasm for the city as we sit in the spring sun at the Puccini café near Waterlooplein.

One of my favourite places is nearby here, Café de Sluyswacht. It's a beautiful old building, dating from 1695, that's leaning over to one side because it's so old – its name tells you that's where the ships would come and be registered at the lock. Not far from there, you'll find the Schreierstoren, the Weeper's Tower. That's where, it's said, the sailors' wives would watch their men leave on the ships setting out to the East Indies – it's really ancient, from 1487! There's a café inside there too, so you can have a drink while you're actually sitting inside a part of Amsterdam's long history.

We locals can sometimes forget to be proud of our city, because we are surrounded by these beautiful canals and buildings all the time.

Partly it's our *'doe maar gewoon...'* thing, ['just be normal...'], which means our culture is about not showing off or being over-proud, and that's fine, as long as we are not too humble. In recent times we've had many great developments in Amsterdam; numerous start-up technical companies, an amazing diversity of cultural events, one of the most highly educated populations of any city worldwide – I could go on! That rich combination of beautiful, ancient surroundings and modern developments is truly something we should be proud of.

That's where I think the *I amsterdam* concept is excellent, because it expresses the role the citizens have to play. The city authorities are focusing on making our cultural climate and creative industries represent Amsterdam, rather than the sex and drugs. Yes, those things exist, but there is so much more to Amsterdam. It has a vibrant heart of creativity.

You'll notice as you wander around the city that there are big renovations happening. These are largely to do with a new metro line connecting the north of the city with the south – which has not proven too popular with locals. Mark has a different view.

Well, the project is taking longer than expected and it causes a lot of upheaval while construction is going on. But most people don't know that the real goal of the metro is to protect the glorious old city in the long term.

Amsterdam must be a part of our dynamic world as a constantly evolving city, not as a museum. We want to attract big international companies to base their HQs here. To do that, we need a balance of the modern and the traditional. By building the metro, we can locate large companies in the south and south-east of the city and give their employees easy access to cultural hotspots as well as to the airport, without spoiling the centre with skyscrapers.

Visitors notice there are far fewer cars in Amsterdam than in most large cities – something we really want to preserve. The huge numbers of bikes help, because cyclists are the ones who truly rule the roads. Cars can't drive fast because the bikes decide what happens on the roads here, and at what speed. The flows of cyclists are almost like the flows of the canals; they direct the shape of the city. You can feel it if you ride on a busy cycle path in the centre. You feel more connected to the real way things are done and how the people behave. But don't follow exactly what the locals do, because they jump red lights all the time. They're the modern day anarchists of Amsterdam!

Mark certainly has the depth of knowledge to understand the true essence of Amsterdam, but I'm surprised when he mentions a very familiar spot for tourists – Vondelpark.

I'm fortunate because I live close to my favorite location. Vondelpark is an amazing place. It stretches from the centre near Leidseplein out to the edge of the city, and it's packed with a diverse range of types. On a sunny day, people are almost naked, lying in the sun. Today you'll find a golf tournament there; you'll always see people walking their dogs, rollerblading, running. And it's safe too – my wife often cycles through the park in the middle of the night with no problem. It feels like this is a place where you can really be yourself.

Between our first talk and the final development of this book, Mark took on the position of head of the Westergasfabriek, Amsterdam's hottest cultural centre. It perfectly suits his passion for promoting the city's cultural qualities.

When I heard about this role, my initial thought was, *Great, that's a creative and special place.* I'd been here as a customer many times; watching movies at Het Ketelhuis cinema, seeing art or fashion events in the Machinegebouw building, and in the past few years I always felt something was really happening at the Westergasfabriek.

Amsterdam has an attitude of re-using what we built in the past, and that is seen in this area's history too. The factory was developed as a gasworks 130 years ago. When there was no longer a need for it, we took the buildings and made something new and exciting out of them. It's now a place where companies with a cultural focus can come and enjoy a good environment to work in, as well as being the venue for big music shows or smaller niche presentations of creativity.

There was, and still is, no master plan. We don't say, "This is how it will be in 2020" in terms of the types of companies or events that we house. As Director, I prefer to see it develop in an organic way, so that we reflect what is happening in Amsterdam, and allow creative co-incidence to develop our plans. Equally, we have to stick to our core values, one of which is collaboration. I encourage the companies that are based here to work together wherever possible,

to keep their doors open and to see how they might help each other by being part of the Westergasfabriek.

A good example of our spirit is Het Ketelhuis. The originators came in the late '90s with an idea and virtually no money. The Westergasfabriek gave them a space and plenty of time to find their feet, because Het Ketelhuis was based on a cultural idea that they adhered to: presenting Dutch movies. They do show other types of films, but Dutch film-making is their focus and core value, and we respected that. Over a decade on, they have three intimate cinema halls, a wonderful café and a great atmosphere, with most of the work done by volunteers. It's important that such creative ideas have the time and space to flourish, and that's an essential role of the Westergasfabriek.

I'm a lucky man too, because I leave my home near Vondelpark and cycle to my work next to Westerpark – two of the city's most attractive green spaces. It's fun to be a park-hopper in Amsterdam!

www.westergasfabriek.nl

THERE WAS THIS LITTLE ECO-SYSTEM
OF DRUG DEALERS, STAG PARTIES,
PROSTITUTES AND OFFICE WORKERS

Most of us have been on a drab city tour with a guide who has clearly done the same show four times that day already. I came across Larae during one of her unique custom-designed trips, which reveal a few extra layers of the city's intriguing story. A genuine love for Amsterdam and fascination with its quirks sparked Larae's decision to take on her 'Amsterdamsel' pseudonym and become a tour guide for curious travellers.

LARAE MALOOLY

AMSTERDAMMER SINCE 2005
CREATOR OF 'AMSTERDAMSEL TOURS' AND 'ORIGINAL AMSTERDAM WALKS'
FAVOURITE AMSTERDAM LOCATION — NIEUWMARKT

The first room I rented was on Oudezijds Voorburgwaal, near the Oude Kerk in the Red Light District. I remember calling my mum from the balcony overlooking the church, and she asked me, "How's the new place?" I could hardly tell her I was looking at a row of prostitutes' windows! So I answered, "It's the oldest neighbourhood in town, there's a church right across the street, it's very safe because there are lots of police." Just at that moment, a loud fight broke out. "What's that?" she asked. "Oh, just a little disturbance, nothing to worry about." Then I saw a group of men looking up at me, making a money gesture and I said, "Mum, I'll call you back."

I had this little eco-system in front of me; drug dealers, stag parties, prostitutes and office workers all intermingled. I'd see the business guys check into the gay Anco Hotel in their suits and then come out wearing leather. Fantastic! Meanwhile, there was a famous actor living down the street, and grannies with their little lace curtains living above the red light windows. I watched different segments of society living close to each other very comfortably, a definite strong point of Amsterdam.

This gave me a big first impression of the diversity my new home town had to offer. Becoming a tour guide was a natural extension of my fascination with the city. As soon as I arrived, I found myself asking numerous questions – why are these canals here? Why do the buildings look this way? Why can I talk in a student café with a 70 year-old opera singer about sex? That openness of Amsterdammers made me stop editing my thoughts, something I didn't even know I was doing until I came here.

Doing tours with teenagers forces you to be creative. With them, I tell a lot about music, about how The Beatles and The Red Hot Chili Peppers spent time here. I also include a lot of interactive exercises, like asking the youngsters to become a neo-Gothic church, to turn their bodies into flying buttresses. Maybe it sounds odd, but they seem to like it! I've also designed an interactive 'World War II and Jewish Amsterdam Tour'. The students are given identity cards, as Jews were in the '40s, but with the names of people who were involved in the Dutch resistance movement. When we arrive at the relevant site, I call out their names, and they read their profiles and act out something related to real events.

It's easy to surprise visitors with places like Java Eiland – they can't believe the land there has all been reclaimed. The older and grungier side of Amsterdam is interesting for tourists too. Perhaps the best example is Wynand Fockink, next to the Krasnapolsky hotel. It's a tiny, cramped bar attached to a distillery, where you can taste all kinds of *jenever*, a traditional Dutch spirit. It's been there since 1679 and was restored in the '90s by some squatters to reflect how it originally looked. And with a name like Fockinck, there are always a few jokes.

Amsterdam is teaching me a lot. I've become much more resilient through dealing with cycling in the wind with rain flying at me at a 45-degree angle, being challenged by the language, and even simple, practical things like having to drag groceries up four or five flights of stairs. Where I come from, back in Texas, you drive; the furthest you might walk is the ten feet from your car to your front door!

www.amsterdamsel.com, www.originalamsterdamwalks.com

RIVER AMSTEL

Take a bicycle and head along this waterway that gave Amsterdam its name, and you'll reach the beautiful village of Ouderkerk aan de Amstel. Looking east, you'll see the impressive Arena stadium, home to Amsterdam's premier football club and second home to Sjaak Swart.

AJAX'S SUCCESS IN THE '60s AND '70s WAS FUELED BY OYSTERS AND VAN DOBBEN KROKETTEN

SJAAK SWART

AMSTERDAMMER SINCE THE 1950'S
PLAYED HIGHEST NUMBER OF GAMES EVER FOR AJAX
FAVOURITE AMSTERDAM LOCATION – AJAX ARENA STADIUM

In the early '70s, Dutch football was absolute king in Europe, and Ajax of Amsterdam was at the very top. Three European Cup triumphs were the won by a squad of players known as *'Het Gouden Ajax'* [The Golden Ajax].

What I remember as a boy, just beginning to develop my own addiction to the sport, was hearing the Dutch players being interviewed on British TV. It was astonishing to hear these foreign players speaking our language, communicating with a greater finesse than any English footballer was capable of at the time. They were classy on and off the field.

Even if you have little interest in football, you will probably have heard about Johan Cruijff, the most famous footballer and coach Holland has ever produced. Yet despite spending many successful years at Ajax, he is not the most adored player in the club's history. That emotion is reserved for Sjaak Swart, a man whose life in the city has always been so completely focused around Ajax – the only club he played for during his entire career – that he is simply known as 'Mr. Ajax'.

Sjaak played during an era when players came from the town where their club was based, and almost everything he has to say about Amsterdam is related to Ajax. That devotion has resulted in his being honoured more than any other Dutchman. He's been knighted by the Queen, made an honorary member *[erelid]* of both Ajax and the National Football Association, and he's an honorary citizen of Amsterdam. With twenty winner's medals at national and international level, he's likely never to be surpassed in the hearts of Ajax supporters.

I met him at the aptly named training ground, De Toekomst – meaning 'The Future'. While Sjaak Swart is a legend of the past, he's a regular face at the coaching pitch in the present; advising and laying the ground for the great teams he hopes are soon to come.

They say I played 600 times for the club, but I think it's closer to 800; all the friendlies I was part of are often forgotten. And since I retired, I've played on average around 40 games per year, so maybe I appeared in more games than any other player in the world. [I do a quick calculation, and it comes to over 2,500 matches! He could well be right.]

My Amsterdam life has been all about Ajax. Back when the old stadium, De Meer, was situated in the Watergraafsmeer area, I lived within a few hundred metres of it, and so did Johan Cruijff and Piet Keizer – we all grew up almost in sight of the ground. Ajax was my family and I didn't ever want anything more than to play for the club.

These days I go to the club's training ground every day. For the past 18 years I've worked with Søren Lerby – he used to play for Ajax too. We coach and advise the players. Even on Saturdays, when the young kids are playing, I like to come and watch.

As we discuss Sjaak's opinions of Amsterdam, the subject continually turns to football and his only club. Even when discussing general impressions of the city, he never fails to return to stories about Ajax.

As a player, I did have a couple of offers to go to other clubs and countries. I never took them because I didn't want to leave my city – though when I finished with Ajax, I did get one very interesting offer.

I was 35 years old in 1973 and we had a player called Johnny Rep coming through in my position, just 18 years old at the time. The club had told me they wanted to develop him, which I could understand, but I couldn't accept sitting on the bench – I never sat on the bench in my career! I thought to myself, *It's better that I finish while I'm at the top.* I was still very fit though, and I'd had a good season – in seven games I had scored the winning goal. We won the European Cup for the third time in a row, and afterwards the club gave me a memorable farewell game. The stadium was full – 60,000 supporters – and it felt like half the city was there! All the best-known singers from Amsterdam came afterwards – Tante Leen, Johnny Jordaan – and we had a huge party that lasted until 6 am the following day. It was the greatest finish to a career you could possibly hope for.

That summer, George Knobel became the new Ajax coach and he told me, "I want you to play another season." Well, I couldn't do that after such a farewell party, could I? Nevertheless, I still felt in good condition, and I was offered a two-year contract with Alkmaar club AZ67, based just 45 kilometres north from here. It was very tempting to play for another team and yet still live in Amsterdam, but I couldn't do it. I simply couldn't! If you play for a club over 800 times, it feels like a betrayal to appear in another club's shirt.

Johan Cruijff played his final season in Holland for Ajax's arch-rivals, Feyenoord, and for a moment I wonder if this might be a criticism of him – but Sjaak is simply not that kind of person. He reminds me of my grandfather; a straight and honest man, respected by all.

In the late '80s, Ajax's De Meer stadium was in disrepair and it was decided that a brand-new arena should be built in the south-east of the city. I expected Sjaak to criticise that move, because to me it feels like the club can't be as connected to the city as it used to be. He's reluctant to say anything negative about his club, yet he does miss that tight connection between club and city.

With the stadium so close to the centre, it meant the club was integral to the city. As players, we felt like we were simply a part of the people of Amsterdam and we lived our lives among them. For example, before games we would go to Leidseplein and sit at the Oesterbar, eating oysters and Van Dobben *kroketten* [the most popular fried snack in Holland]. Locals used to walk past and shout to us, "Hey, Sjakie, have a good game" or "Johan, score a goal for me!" After eating, we'd ride our bikes to the stadium, where we'd play in front of those same people. You could say that Van Dobben kroketten fueled Ajax's success of the '60s and '70s! It was a different feeling, like a family – we were from the city and the club was a real part of Amsterdam.

You can't imagine that now. Players can't just wander around in the centre because they will get chased by fans, and everything is arranged for them at the club. When I played, my wife would clean my shirts, and we cycled everywhere. Now even a 19 year-old player has a Mercedes and wouldn't dream of washing his own jersey. Okay, times change and you have to adapt, but I think we had an extra motivation to play well for the locals, because we were locals ourselves.

We keep the old ideals of a football family alive though. Eighteen years ago, some former players created Lucky Ajax, perhaps the only club of its type. If you play 100 games for Ajax, you can join us. Sometimes Dennis Bergkamp plays, Ronald Koeman, the De Boer brothers. We make sure the spectators can come and talk with the team. It's great fun and I still play too. Yes, I know, I'm nearly 74 now, and I don't have the same speed as those young players, but I can still beat them with my technique, and I can still find them with a 40-metre pass! It's impossible for me to stop – I'm addicted to football.

Sjaak can remember details of almost every major game he played. I mention that I was born in 1967 and he immediately jumps in.

We played a great game against Liverpool in '67 at Amsterdam's Olympic Stadium! That was the first time a team from the Netherlands had beaten an English team, and the final score was 5-1. We were semi-professionals in those days and always believed those British clubs were stronger than us, so it was a big psychological breakthrough. Nobody could see a thing because the weather was foggy, but I played my game and made four assists during the match. That was the beginning of a real change in Ajax; when we started to believe we could do something special.

By 1973, we were at our peak. We played against Bayern München in the quarter-finals of the European Cup. Beckenbauer was the big man of Bayern, and over the next three years, they were champions of Europe. But that year, with eight players from the German national team in their squad, we beat them 4-0 in front of 50,000 supporters. We played so well that we just kept the ball for the last 10 minutes. It was the ultimate in 'total football' – switching positions, surging up the field and crowding them out of the ball. We drove the Germans crazy with our game, in a way that they'll never forget. We found that out when Jopie [Cruijff] had his testimonial finale five years later. He had asked Bayern to come and play, and they killed us!

Normally in a benefit game, you play at a reasonable level and put on a show for the fans, but you allow the other team to play well and win, maybe 4-3 or something. Instead, they came and ran like hell – it was their chance to avenge that defeat – and they tackled Johan, kicked him and won 8-0. Really, 8-0!

I've watched the highlights of that game on YouTube and it's painful. The Ajax guys clearly saw it as a fun event, but the Bayern players meant business. Renowned player Karl-Heinz Rummenigge apologised for it in an interview a few years later.

These days, Swart gets his enjoyment from coaching players for the Amsterdam side. His mobile phone rings; it's a player from his coaching past who is now playing in Turkey.

He was asking me if I could help him find a club in the Dutch league. A lot of my former players still call me later in their careers. I try to get close to them as individuals when coaching, so we know each other very well. The first quality I look for in a footballer is technique. Then it's important how fast he is in the first metres, plus he needs the overview of the game. Most of all, he must be good in his mind and his attitude; I work a lot with them on this part too.

One player we are coaching now has all the skills the great players from the '70s had. Nevertheless, he's not making it. You know, for half an hour he's good, and for the rest of the game he's sleeping. If he doesn't get the ball for a while, he just gives up. When I was playing, if my teammates weren't passing to me, I'd shout at them and scream for the ball. He just says, "Okay, I don't care" and switches off. I've spoken to him again and again about this. I tell him what a great life he can have as a footballer; he just has to improve his attitude.

I've been lucky because I helped develop some of the recent Dutch World Cup team – Rafael van der Vaart, Wesley Sneijder. Ajax is the kind of club that always produces new talent, because we focus on coaching the players from a young age and try to develop their technique and mentality. It's hard for the club, because when they get to around 21, they want to go and earn the big money in England, Spain, Italy. But I hope we will grow a new team that can at least play in the UEFA Champions League every year, and maybe become European champions again. That's my dream.

A familiar-looking guy walks towards us and greets Sjaak with a warm neck-hold. He's introduced as Cornelis, the brother of Martin Jol, who was coach of Ajax at the time of our meeting, and he tells us what people really think about Sjaak.

"They say that Johan Cruijff was big – and of course, that's true," explains Cornelis. "But HE is bigger. Sjaak stayed loyal to the club his whole career, he never said a bad thing about them, and when they lost he was almost sick with it. Johan was big, yes, but Sjaak Swart *is* Mr. Ajax."...

www.esselsoccer.nl

WESTERPARK

One of Amsterdam's beautiful green spaces, the Westerpark, backs onto the Westergasfabriek, a former gasworks that now houses cafés and cultural events. It's also where Fya Hopelezz regularly hangs out.

THE GAY COMMUNITY IS AN IMPORTANT PART OF THE CITY. AMSTERDAM SHOULD ALWAYS BE A SAFE PLACE FOR ANYONE WHO IS DIFFERENT

FYA HOPELEZZ

AMSTERDAMMER SINCE 1994
GAY RIGHTS ACTIVIST, FIRE AND LIGHT PERFORMANCE ARTIST
FAVOURITE AMSTERDAM LOCATION — WESTERPARK

How do you combine glamour, activism and fire-eating performance art? You do it by being the dynamo that is Fya Hopelezz.

She's one of those born leaders who hold no formal authority. Yet she's followed because of her integrity and the way she stands up for a valuable cause. The banner *Right to Feel Safe'* is a one-woman movement that drove thousands of people onto the streets to say they wanted a safer city and violence against the gay community in Amsterdam to stop.

I attended the protest, which culminated in a gathering at the Homomonument by the Westerkerk, the 17th-century church on the Prinsengracht. Fya stood before the crowd, 30 years young and brimming with attitude and a passion for the truth. She delivered her message powerfully, with utter precision: "We're here, we're fucking queer, get used to it!" A minute later, the crowd sang the words back to her, an echo of their uncrowned queen.

It was a genuine hair-standing-on-the-neck moment.

Over the following months, I got to know Fya and became enthralled by her vigour, conviction and intelligence. Despite an early end to her education, she speaks Egyptian and can tell you about almost every religion on the planet. She reads for hours every day, sleeps for just a few hours at night and takes the world on with an attitude that simply says, "I will do it."

As I write, Fya is performing her fire and light act in New York, with her own unique look and style. If she stays there, she'll be one of many who have come and gone from Amsterdam, which is historically a crossroads and still is today. Special individuals like Fya, who have such an intensity, leave their mark indelibly.

Meet the indefatigable and incomparable Fya Hopelezz.

I was born in Alkmaar, 45 km to the north, and moved here when I was 14. It's not such a great story – I was kicked out of the house – but that gave me the chance to go to Amsterdam and I took it. I always knew I would come here, ever since I was four years old, when my parents used to take me shopping on Sundays. I loved to see these punks with piercings, the odd and unusual characters – I was captivated by all that even then.

We sit on the terrace outside Pacific Parc café on a typical Dutch summer's day – meaning cloudy, with moments of sunshine. Nobody ever comes to Amsterdam because of the weather. Fya's reason was simply that she is different.

I came out as a lesbian soon after arriving; it was made easier by the way the gay community is very much an important part of the city. Amsterdam should be like that; a safe place for anyone who is different, in whatever way. Unfortunately that's not always the case, and in 2004 my girlfriend and I got beaten up. Strangely, that led to me opening a lesbian bar.

The attack left me so traumatised I couldn't go to school, where I was studying Leisure Management. My tutor helped by offering to grade me on an assignment about creating a business focused on the gay community. I later borrowed money on the basis of my project and that's how the 'Sugarbar' started.

When I hear those stories, I want to say, "That's Amsterdam – city of opportunity, people turning adversity into action." But I've heard different opinions on that, so I'm interested in what someone like Fya has to say.

I do think it's a place of opportunities and yes, you can be and do anything if you want it enough. But you have to be persistent and come up with an idea that's different. We labelled the Sugarbar an 'open-minded lesbian bar' and naturally our target audience was primarily lesbians, but everybody would be welcome. We wanted the gay community to integrate with the regular community, especially in the Jordaan area, where they are quite tolerant towards difference. It's ironic that the beating was the reason I opened the bar. I felt, *Screw you! This is my city. I'll put myself even more in your face!*

We meet the day before a September protest, which Fya created from scratch; a five-day Facebook-promoted campaign that would result in thousands taking to the streets to demonstrate against incidents of violence against gay people in Amsterdam.

I've had some experience with politicians here and it can be difficult to push them into taking action on behalf of minorities. Yet as soon as the media catch hold of something, the politicians suddenly wake up. Nobody contacted us at all about the protest, until this morning, when it was in Amsterdam newspaper *Het Parool* that we're going ahead in tomorrow. All of a sudden I get emails from the police department, from the mayor, from everyone – all wanting to participate in the protest to show how much they care! It's ridiculous.

Perhaps the political system of the Netherlands doesn't fit the capital. Amsterdammers are quite different from the rest of the country; residents are much more radical here than in the smaller towns. At times I have this crazy idea that Amsterdam should be a state with its own political system. New Yorkers are the same – they don't feel American, they feel like New Yorkers!

Amsterdammers have always said, "I'll do what I want and I'll let you do what you want – and if I don't like you, I just won't talk to you." They have a profound sense of 'I want to be who I want to be and that's the real essence of this city – strong, resilient people. It doesn't matter what the buildings are like, Amsterdammers make the city what it is.

I go inside to order more coffee and notice the amazing chandelier at the Pacific Parc. It's like a flying machine out of a Terry Gilliam movie. Armed with caffeine again, I ask Fya about some of the other prejudices surrounding some recent incidents.

The public is misinformed by the media. They're told that Moroccans are carrying out all the violence against gays, but that's not accurate. The media might like to believe that, but prejudice is not acted on only by immigrants. People are discriminating against Muslims in such a horrible way and then blaming *them* for being discriminatory. The only ones who are getting bashed more than gays are Moroccans and other Muslims.

I get calls from the media because I had been a victim of hate crime. They ask me, "Were you attacked by Muslims?" When I say no, the phone goes dead. The reality? The media are there to sell stories, not to represent any cause or minority. As a result of my activism, the bar, being beaten up, I've seen what goes on behind the curtain – and it's not always good.

It's a thrill to be sitting with somebody who moves others in the interests of a cause. I get drawn into Fya's focus on issues and feel my own need to stand up, become involved.

I never used to call myself an activist. In the past, the attitude to that was, 'Oh, there she goes again, typical dyke', but now it's starting to become popular again. My activism began when I was beaten up. It made me was so angry, because these guys were arrested and then they were all released the same night! I was furious that I couldn't be safe in my own city.

That gave me this profound feeling of, *This is my city* and even made me love Amsterdam even more. Starting the Sugarbar was as much a statement as anything else. I also organised some lesbian parties and wrote some pieces for various gay magazines, mostly about being beaten up and how I felt about it. Then I started performing, often with some kind of message in my shows – like arriving naked wrapped only in a gay flag. More recently, when a friend got beaten up, it sparked me to think, *Not again! I have to do something now.*

The last protest in June was bigger than any other in recent years because I focused on making it that way. I'm happy to sit behind my computer for 24 hours and send out press notices. I'll call whoever I need to until I get the support and I'll keep going until I get a "yes" – I don't give a fuck! I don't do things halfway.

We take a look at Fya's performance photos on Facebook. She's developed amazing costumes and a dramatic act.

I was running the bar and while watching the acts I'd booked, I always thought, *Jesus, I can do better than that and I'm paying for this!* It started at a friend's birthday party, where I did a simple dance show, and it went on from there. I do have a unique type of performance; it's different from the regular fire-shows of guys with black leather pants blowing a few flames. I think you have to consider all aspects of your performance – how you look can be as important as what you do.

My costumes are generally put together quite cheaply because I find stuff that I can sew and combine to create a new image. There's no point in looking like everyone else, so my costumes are all my own handmade designs. The make-up? Well, I picked up all kinds of tricks from the drag queens, darling!

The dream is to make it as a performer, which is why I work damn hard at it. Hopefully it looks natural when I'm onstage, but I train at least four hours a day because the only way to make it great is through practice, and I never stop.

In the weeks following our meeting, Fya spends time doing gigs in New York. Locals stop her on 7th Avenue saying, "Hey, you're the fire girl!" Her extrovert character finds a second home, but Amsterdam still draws her back.

I want to live in New York for a while, but there are some really special places that will always bring me back to Amsterdam. Westerpark and the Westergasfabriek are the future of the city for me; big concerts, lots of restaurants, three clubs, the Ketelhuis cinema and this café, Pacific Parc. It's also a very mixed area of the city in terms of ethnicity and wealth.

The Jordaan area is cool too because the most down-to-earth characters live there and it's just gorgeous – like you're in a little village within Amsterdam. Everybody knows each other. It's cute.

Especially on the gay level, Amsterdam is a special place, although I worry about the changes in atmosphere. We were the first city in which gay couples could get married and Job Cohen was the first person in the world to marry same-sex couples *[see Cohen's interview on page 126]*. That helps the perception of Amsterdam as a gay capital, as did the gay community taking to the streets in the '70s and '80s. They fought really hard for their rights, and historically we've been front-runners in a lot of areas. Sometimes, though, we take things for granted and forget that we have to keep the voice of the minorities heard. So I'm always gonna stay loud!

A construction machine trundles towards our table with a dangerously sharp-edged piece of equipment sticking over the side, and I warn Fya to watch out. "I thought you were going to get stabbed!"

Or someone from the city council put a contract on me? "Get that girl, but make it look like an accident, and maybe then she'll shut up!"

www.invents.nl

CANAL SKYLINE

Amsterdam's unique group of artists always leave you needing a second look. Marcel Ozymantra is no exception.

DON'T GO THROUGH RED LIGHTS ON YOUR BIKE BECAUSE THE LOCALS DO. YOU'LL GET MESSED UP

MARCEL OZYMANTRA

AMSTERDAMMER SINCE 1993

ARTIST AND POET, AUTHOR OF NOVEL, 'AAN TRAAGHEID ONTKOMEN' [ESCAPE FROM INDOLENCE]

FAVOURITE AMSTERDAM LOCATION – CAFÉ DE BUURVROUW

Amsterdammers' level-headed attitude towards fame has surely influenced its ability to accommodate all kinds of artists, well known or otherwise. There is a history of city-sponsored subsidies to enable artists to focus more on their work and less on earning a living to pay the bills.

Recently those subsidies have decreased, yet there is still an attraction for creatives such as Marcel Ozymantra to set up their studios in odd corners of Amsterdam. (Yes, Ozymantra really is the name he goes by. Just be careful how you ask him about it; he's not too willing to discuss the subject.)

Go to the Oude Kerk in the city centre and you might find Marcel taking money for entrance tickets or generally sorting things out. He does that three days a week, while his main focus is creating unusual art through painting, poetry and prose. His is the archetypal 'struggling artist' story.

You won't find him despondent or short of an opinion though, as he has firm views on the changes in recent years, both to his chosen city of Amsterdam, and to the art world of which he is as much a part as anyone.

Who knows, in years to come tourists may visit the Ozymantra museum. Alternatively, he'll continue to work in relative obscurity.

After talking to him, I'm pretty sure which one he'd prefer.

" I grew up in Het Gooi, the rich region south-east of Amsterdam. I must admit, I'm glad I got out of there. It's mostly comfortable for those who are trying to, well, die slowly. Sometimes when I return to visit family there, I notice how people walk around like zombies, going through the motions. I always miss the energy of the city.

We sit in Marcel's third-floor apartment as he smokes handmade roll-ups. His attitude towards the towns immediately outside of Amsterdam is similar to that of many city dwellers – they tend to see these as farmland or homes for affluent retirees. Marcel is a true artist who draws from a city's creativity.

When I first arrived in Amsterdam, I studied to teach drawing, although the real reason I went to that school was to learn how to create comic books. While studying, I realised that painting was much more fun, and I began to write more poetry too. When I finished school, I started to write prose. I guess my life is at its best when I am doing something creative.

Unemployment benefit was still available for artists when my study finished – maybe I was one of the last to get it. I told them, "I'm an artist and there's no chance of a job to pay the rent." They said, "Yeah, that's okay, take it easy." So I received that for three or four years while I developed my painting style and writing. After that, I got an artist's benefit that covers three quarters of what you need and gradually, of course, I had to start working.

Amongst other things, I found a job in the logistics department of a newspaper, where I had to put letters in envelopes in a certain order. I managed to stick at for two years, from 8 am to 4 pm, listening to Arrow Radio all day – you know, the classic-rock station. That's when I found out what a real job is, and with every passing day, I went slightly crazier.

Now I work at the Oude Kerk for three days a week as a concierge; I have almost no money but a lot of free time to focus on my art.

Looking around Marcel's place, I see pieces of his work everywhere. Half-finished canvasses propped up below finished pieces hung on walls; scraps and scribbles of poetry on the table. He seems diffident yet never stopping his art – Amsterdam gives you the space for that.

One of the most attractive aspects here is that the art world is really non-central. There are a few areas with some medium-sized galleries clustered together, plus the few very important museums, but they tend not to show work of local up-and-coming artists; you have to be established first to be a part of the 'official' art circuit.

Separately, you have the 'unofficial' part – the Sunday painters and the aspiring semi-professionals like me, and there's a whole range of medium-sized and small galleries where you may show your art. In New York I was very impressed by the art world's structure, which may be as decentralised as Amsterdam's, but of course it's a bigger city with more money. In our city the art is more creative in a small

THE ART IN A SMALL GALLERY IN AMSTERDAM IS MORE CREATIVE THAN IN A BIG GALLERY IN NEW YORK

gallery than it is in a big NYC gallery.

Amsterdam has always been a place for creatives, although there is a change taking place. There used to be a lot of space and a good attitude towards artists, but there is a feeling now that they are being taken for granted. I sense a new point of view developing: "You want to do your art? Go ahead, no problem. Sorry? You want money? Don't be silly!" And competition is tough here, because there are so many artists who have been attracted by Amsterdam's aura and reputation.

In the background, one of Marcel's many CDs is playing and the song sounds like a wood saw. Then I realise there actually is some machinery grinding away in the background nearby. It's a sign of how unusual he is that I wouldn't have been at all surprised if his music taste included such noise. Marcel holds cutting opinions on artistic issues and on why the Amsterdam creative world is changing.

The 'why?' is the most difficult! Probably it's because the rules have been continually breached since the '60s. Tolerance was the main focus, not rules; things became freer and freer. That's fine for the ones who can stand that kind of freedom, who can manage the boundaries. But there are a lot of people, drawn like flies to honey, thinking, *Freedom – that's an excuse to do anything I want.*

The squatters' movement was a great thing in the '70s and '80s, even the '90s. Big empty buildings were overtaken and became a great environment for people to go and exchange experiences. Music venues like Paradiso and OT301 were originally squats, which turned into cultural centres thanks to the creative individuals living there within the liberal legal framework of the time.

Later in the '90s, a lot of southern Europeans thought it would be nice to live in Amsterdam, and the drugs, of course, also attracted them. They went into squatting with a different attitude, one that annoyed a lot of Amsterdammers. Those from the Netherlands were looking for a permanent place to live, as well as their freedom, so they created a very artsy and socialist community. Those coming from outside didn't have that same feeling of ownership, but rather the summer holiday feeling of 'trash the place and move on'.

The original ideal behind squatting was to cause an almost anarchic state. That came from the punk movement; big ideals that were not workable within the confines of a society were involved. For a while it worked very well, because society in Amsterdam was so loose. Now the city authorities go the opposite direction and completely prohibit squatting!

Similar changes are happening in the area of soft drugs. Marijuana was tolerated, but the authorities never intended big shops and businesses to be created as a result. Rather, it was an attempt to get soft drugs out of the illegal environment, meaning; if you wanted to consume it yourself, or produce it for you and your friends, that was okay. Now it's become so commercial, they want to rein it in.

Many have said to me, "The essence of Amsterdam is that I am free to be myself." Marcel is sceptical.

This whole freedom thing... There is a limit to what society can handle as freedom, and what an individual or commercial entity wants as freedom. The balance here in Amsterdam has been totally lost. A lot of people, when they come to Amsterdam, notice that they can be freer than where they come from, even now. But that's because they were brought up 'properly, with proper rules' in their society – so they already have limits inside their heads. Then they come to a place where the limits are way beyond their own.

There's a whole generation in Amsterdam with no proper upbringing at all; everything was possible from the beginning. Then you get a very different approach to this freedom thing.

It's true that the city is becoming more controlled, but still, it's freer than most cities. Nevertheless, certain things seem to have changed permanently. For example, in the '90s you could still spot a lot of characters wearing alternative dress. That's totally gone now. Today you might see one person in gothic dress, maybe another with coloured hair and, if you're lucky, a hippie. There's a much more formalised way of dressing – still casual, but more suits are appearing. That's a simple but significant sign of change.

There used to be a lot of characters drawing attention to themselves with their clothing because they wanted to make a statement about themselves as an individual. In the past 10 years, that statement has changed to, "I want to be part of the large crowd." It's still more casual here than in most countries, but even casual clothing can become a uniform after a while.

We take a break and wander upstairs to Marcel's attic-studio. There are countless tubes of oil paint and brushes scattered around, and the walls are dashed with daubs of colour where canvasses have been positioned while he creates. We discuss how explicit art's meaning should be.

If you write down a description of a visual artistic statement, the art simply becomes what it says. That leaves no freedom for a different interpretation. For example, write, 'Stop violence' and that's it, nothing left to the imagination. Alternatively, you can also make the kind of movie Sam Peckinpah used to make, showing violence that gets under a person's skin; maybe urging him to stop violence but also giving the chance to think about it, to relate to it, to relate to victims. That's much more involved in the mind. It's not a slogan. Art is not a slogan – except, I suppose, when Andy Warhol does it...

I consider myself like a mother when making my art. The moment it gets born into the world is the moment the starts to live by connecting with the audience. When the viewer sees it, they have their own ideas and feelings about it; they connect to the piece and it starts to live more. That makes the whole slogan thing very empty.

Marcel's creativity doesn't know where to stop and his 'very Amsterdam' novel is due to be published at the end of 2011.

It's about a coffee shop! You could say the main character is the coffee shop; a customer becomes involved with the people there, and develops a very paranoid illusion. Probably they'll like it in the USA. I also write poetry and regularly blog about my painting and appreciation for other artists' work. There's no point for me just sticking to painting or sculpture, because I'm interested in and inspired by all kinds of creative media.

Working at the Oude Kerk, in the heart of the Red Light District, Marcel has a unique view on the Redlight Fashion project and the changes in the area in general.

I think it's disturbing, a sign of ever-more conservative times. There's this area, the centre of the seedy part of Amsterdam life, which many avoid because they think of it as disgusting and immoral – but it's also exciting to be there exactly for that reason. Suddenly they put that fashion stuff there, which is supposed to give the area some decency to attract so-called 'design tourists'. They walk past the artistic stuff and are suddenly confronted with the hookers – then the hookers are taken out of context, because it appears normal that you have the fashion side by side with prostitutes; the women become part of the display.

The authorities try to make it a respectable area, but they simply push the sex workers away to the outer, shady areas. This can be seen as a good and politically correct idea, but perhaps the city planners forget that many tourists don't come to Amsterdam for the nice art, the lovely canals or the beautiful buildings. They come for the drugs and the prostitution. That is reality. And do the city authorities really think prostitution stops just because there's no window to sell from?

Balance can be a scary thing. I don't like the mix of regular and criminal cultures. Seeing a bit of art, a bit of fashion, then a prostitute, as if it's normal – I find it disrespectful to the women working for their

money. It's not a great life they lead; they are in business supplying a demand and they are human beings. You can argue that they're being degraded anyway, but there's no need to make it worse.

He clearly has some frustration with trends in Amsterdam. Even when talking about the good things, Marcel struggles to keep his dissatisfaction at bay.

I can't say I'm happy there are a lot of tourists here, but I do earn my living as a result, so I have to accept it. I tell them, "Stick to the rules as you know them at home; don't act as if you know the rules of this city. Don't walk on bike paths because Amsterdammers do it. Don't go through red lights because others do, because you mess it up and you get messed up. And watch out for the locals, they will drive their bikes right through you!" You see visitors wandering around stoned, not realising that locals work here, live here. They're not waiting for you to get out of the way.

A positive feature of the art world in Amsterdam is the active participation of artists themselves. Marcel has a strong connection with the Radar gallery, at Rozengracht 77.

The owner, a friend of mine, wanted to open a gallery and show my stuff there, so I got very much involved in building it up and helping him with the legal stuff. We went to all kinds of galleries together to see how it's done, so that I could help in the early stages. Now he's managing it himself.

In New York, they have their galleries hidden away in the back of big buildings, so you have to go inside and take the elevator, which I find really weird. Here, a place like Radar is on a busy street and you can just wander in. It's easy to be intimidated by a gallery; someone entering may think, *Art, white space, quiet; it's not my world.* There's also that thought of *I should say something smart, I should look smart.* Amsterdammers are likely to have a counter-reaction to that atmosphere and will happily say out loud, "What a pretentious lot!"

You shouldn't care about whether people feel it's pretentious or intimidating because, truth be told, proper art probably works best when it *is* a touch elitist, when it is difficult to approach. It's a psychological thing. If you tell someone, "This painting costs 50 euros", they think that's too much for a piece of paper and some paint. If you tell them it's 750 or 1,500 euros, they become interested because they wonder why the hell it's so expensive.

Obviously I'd love to make a lot of money from my art and be able to charge those prices, but that's not important for me. If I could give my work away for nothing and still have enough money to live, I wouldn't mind. I think I'm a bit old-fashioned; I would like to be considered part of this highly revered group of artists, most of whom are dead! So I guess I'll have to wait until I'm dead too.

It's silly to expect some kind of reward for your art. If I want to make money, I have to make the work that everybody wants and make more noise in selling myself. But I make my kind of art because I like it. I think I'm good at it and it gives my life a bit more sense, having the feeling that I am producing something. I don't like the vegetative life of simply existing. This is an adventure in itself, a challenge.

Naturally the name 'Ozymantra' attracts curiosity and it's no different in my case. When I ask, "Is it your real name?" Marcel answers with a very curt, "Nope." I feel the need to dig a bit further.

All right, I needed a good Internet handle, something memorable. It's maybe a bit too outgoing in some ways. You know how the Dutch are. "Don't talk immediately about yourself", "Keep it real, keep it in perspective, don't rise above the grass," and stuff like that. It's kind of tricky to use a name that does exactly the opposite, but perhaps that's my intention.

I don't have to do anything to be remembered; the name in itself already draws attention. And it covers the situation of a kind of **complica**ted **person.**

www.ozymantra.nl
www.radar-amsterdam.com

THE FILM I'M MOST PROUD OF IS A REAL AMSTERDAM STORY ABOUT A FOREIGNER TRYING TO MAKE HER WAY

SUZANNE RAES

AMSTERDAMMER SINCE 1987
TV AND DOCUMENTARY FILM DIRECTOR
FAVOURITE AMSTERDAM LOCATION – ABOARD THE FERRY CROSSING THE RIVER IJ

I have often wondered why Amsterdam's atmosphere has not attracted more Hollywood producers to use it as a set. Perhaps it's the practicalities. Getting around the canals with trucks full of equipment would certainly be a challenge, and stopping the bikes from riding through the set a near impossibility – cyclists stop for no-one in this city.

One person who has captured the city on film – inside and out – is film maker Suzanne Raes. Some of her documentaries, such as *The Rainbow Warriors of Waiheke Island*, have taken her as far as New Zealand. Others have taken place much closer to home, in the Amsterdam places she has loved for over 20 years.

So what does the city look like through the eyes of a movie director?

"My favourite way of seeing the city is from the other side of the River IJ. If you take the free ferry at the back of the central station to Amsterdam-Noord [North], you can see the relationship between the buildings and the water more clearly. Noord is very different to the main city. A lot of industry used to be based there, but that's changing rapidly. One example is the NDSM, where ships were built in the past. My TV production company, IDTV, has its office there, and a lot of cultural developments are happening around those old buildings.

There are very few high buildings in Amsterdam, so another less familiar view is from high up. The restaurant on the top floor of the central library and the bar on top of the Kalvertoren shopping centre on Kalverstraat are two locations to take pictures from. The canals are beautiful, but I always feel a bit enclosed, and I like to have a focus point that's far away. I enjoy being in these open spaces with a longer view.

Almost every year, Brouwersgracht is voted as Holland's most beautiful canal street. I meet Suzanne at her apartment there, late on a Sunday evening. She's extremely busy, but still makes time to share how she accelerated her start in film-making.

After studying history at the University of Amsterdam and working for a talk show, I went to New York and took some video courses for five months. I loved it there – still miss it sometimes – and Amsterdam felt even more like a village when I returned. All the tall buildings you see here, like the Bimhuis concert hall and the Rembrandttoren, have only been built in the past 15 years, and there are very few of them. That massive skyline and the intensity of New York were an exciting contrast with my smaller home city. But after a few months, you settle back into the 'international village' life of Amsterdam. The calmer pace is a better way to live, long-term.

Amsterdam's also inspiring from a creative point of view. Many small companies I like to work with as an independent film-maker are based here. Most major TV stations are over in Hilversum, just outside of the city, but that's more the broadcasting and machinery behind the industry; the creative part is in Amsterdam. There are lots of studios near the centre for editing, or with colour-grading facilities, so everything's very close by. If we need to do re-titling, for example, I just make a call, and we ride our bikes for 10 minutes and get the job done. I think that would be more difficult in London or New York!

Another advantage of the Netherlands is that you can get subsidies and funding to make cultural documentaries for television. I meet American film-makers who take out a mortgage on their house to finance a film and then try to sell it to one of the major channels. Here it's the other way round – if you can convince a broadcaster to show the film based on your concept, you receive the money first and then make the film.

Suzanne staged a concert for musician Lake Montgomery [see Lake's interview on page 4] in the exact place I am sitting – her living room! She's a willing sponsor of creative individuals, and this characteristic showed itself in the making of her 'most Amsterdam' film.

In my early career, I felt uncomfortable filming situations too close to my own life, but once I made a couple of pieces based in Amsterdam, I became much more connected to my own city.

The film I'm most proud of is *De Huizen van Hristina* [The Houses of Hristina]. It's about an illegal Bulgarian cleaner, scrubbing and vacuuming houses in the centre of Amsterdam. She didn't want to be invisible, so she started photographing the houses she cleaned, as well as herself in those empty houses. It's a real Amsterdam story – a foreigner, trying to make her way, contrasted against the comfortable interiors belonging to established home-owners. She was also my cleaning lady and we worked on the film together; the first shot is from my own house. Hristina's now studying at the Rietveld Art Academy.

So where does a film-maker recommend seeing movies in Amsterdam?

I love the Westerpark, partly because it's such a great open space, and partly because it's next to the Westergasfabriek cultural centre – that's really a part of the essence of the city. You can watch movies at the Ketelhuis there – it's a small cinema and café run by volunteers, typical Amsterdam. Elsewhere, there's Lab 111, which has a great dinner and film programme. Studio/K often has a very unusual set of alternative movies, and Rialto is a small and stylish cinema showing foreign and alternative movies.

At the end of our meeting, Suzanne tells me about her latest project. "I'm making a documentary about De Dijk, an Amsterdam band that's been together for 30 years. Pim's the keyboard player. You should get in contact with him – he takes amazing pictures."

I did contact Pim. And that is how the city photography for this book came about."

www.therainbowwarriors.nl, www.hristinatasheva.com

AMSTERDAM COERCES YOU INTO THINKING ABOUT YOURSELF AND WHAT YOU REALLY WANT TO DO, WHO YOU REALLY ARE

JOB COHEN

AMSTERDAMMER SINCE 2001

LAWYER, POLITICIAN AND FORMER MAYOR OF AMSTERDAM

FAVOURITE AMSTERDAM LOCATION – RIVER AMSTEL

As this book began to develop, I asked a number of residents, "Who is the most influential Amsterdammer of the past decade?"

There was only one man mentioned – Job Cohen, mayor of Amsterdam, 2001–2010. And as they talked about him, it became clear that he was not influential because of his position only, but because of the man he is.

Cohen came into his role at a time when racial tensions in the city were simmering. These frictions boiled to the surface in 2004, when controversial film-maker Theo van Gogh was murdered by a Moroccan Muslim in a kind of ritual killing.

To some it appeared a senseless race crime by the killer, Mohammed Bouyeri, but if you make a film in which words from the Koran are projected onto a woman's naked body – as Theo van Gogh did – you might expect an extreme reaction. Surely no one can ever say it is right to kill, but there were certainly two sides to this story.

The expected rioting and violence after the murder never occurred in Amsterdam, thanks to Cohen's approach to dealing with the different factions. He was voted a 'European Hero' by *Time* magazine in 2005 for his efforts.

I was living in Vienna at the time and had no idea of how things really were in the city. I've read books about that period and as I wondered how the mayor managed to keep things under control, the words *Cohen brought the people together to discuss* kept appearing. Easy to write. How the hell to do it when many are furious and feeling attacked, when prejudice on both sides is brought to the surface? What qualities would you need as a leader and as an individual to manage that?

Besides his involvement in events surrounding that incident, Cohen was also the first public figure to marry same-sex couples, having previously worked on the changes in legislation to allow it. In one highly visible action, covered by the world's media, he broke down huge barriers of prejudice.

In April 2010, Cohen moved on to become leader of the *Partij van de Arbeid* [PvdA], the Dutch labour party. I'd expected it might be difficult to get such a busy man to share his views on the city, yet he immediately liked the idea. Suddenly I found myself in the Dutch Houses of Parliament in The Hague, sitting across the table from a man who is surely the definition of integrity, and an important part of Amsterdam's recent history.

THE CONCEPTS OF SHARES AND SHAREHOLDERS WERE DEVELOPED IN AMSTERDAM IN THE 17TH CENTURY. COMMERCE AND CREATING NEW BUSINESS IS AN IMPORTANT PART OF AMSTERDAM'S HISTORY

Job Cohen at the Gay Parade, pictured together with The Brothers Grimm - icons of Amsterdam's gay scene.

I grew up and studied outside of Amsterdam, but 10 years before I became mayor, we decided to take a second house in Amsterdam. That's because my wife always said, "At least once, I want to live in Amsterdam." We found a place at Herengracht 52, next to the labour party's HQ – purely a co-incidence, but prophetic.

It was a great pleasure to be mayor of this city and I learned about Amsterdam through that role.

Cohen's office is simple and straightforward – typical of the man. As we sit together, I mention my hope of also meeting with politician Ahmed Marcouch. "He's in the building. Let's see if we can get hold of him." His assistant makes the call and then sits with us during our meeting. As Cohen warms to the subject of his favourite city, he jokes with her about her 'unlucky' situation of never having lived in the country's capital.

Amsterdam's openness is based on its history, when business demanded a practical acceptance of different types of people. That openness caused Amsterdam to become a magnet for all of those who want to elaborate on the one thing they're good at, no matter what it might be.

But sometimes that openness can be misinterpreted. I can remember very well one of the members of the city council saying to me, "In Amsterdam a lot is possible, but not everything." That's a very good phrase to help understand the real nature of the city. There have to be boundaries to everything, and although Amsterdam's limits may be looser than in other cities, I believe you still need an element of control.

When I became mayor and had my first press conference, I said it was my ambition to keep things together, *de boel bij elkaar houden*. I said this because I knew that Amsterdam is so multicultural, with nearly 180 different nationalities today... So many different cultures living together, and to a large extent they want to live together here. Most of the time it goes quite smoothly, but I also knew we might face some troubles because immigration was already growing as a political issue across Europe.

I begin to notice something about Cohen that is different from most other politicians I have met. He doesn't calculate his answers before he speaks – rather, he looks you in the eye and shares his opinion about the city and how it's perceived.

Amsterdam is a small city – nobody outside the country believes you when you tell them there are less than one million inhabitants here. If you see what's going on here – all the publishers, the artists, so much diverse music, and so many new businesses – it's unbelievable. I often think that most of the Amsterdammers don't realise how special that really is.

What is the essence of Amsterdam? Firstly, freethinking, and then, creativity. People come here because they say to themselves, *Here I*

have the room and freedom to do what I want, so that I can develop into who I want to be. That feeling comes because nobody looks at you and thinks, *What you're doing is very odd.* Whatever you do, people say, "No problem, go ahead – if you don't harm me, I don't care what you do."

It's the freethinking that makes the creativity possible; it becomes acceptable to do something out of the ordinary. On top of that, of course, you have to earn money, so that's when entrepreneurship emerges, to make valuable use of this creativity. The concepts of shares and shareholders were developed in Amsterdam in the 17th century, so this idea of commerce and creating new business is an important part of Amsterdam's history.

I've often wondered where Cohen's broad-minded approach comes from. Not everyone has an inclusive attitude to society, especially in politics, and I want to know what in his personal history makes him think and behave that way.

I really don't know. Maybe it's something to do with my Jewish background. Well, to be honest, I don't feel very Jewish at all, but of course, I am and it's known that I am. It's true though that my parents told me a lot about the Second World War. I was born two years after it had ended; it wasn't possible for them to have kids any earlier because they were forced into hiding. My maternal grandparents were both killed in the war, so that has its influence too. Or maybe my approach is connected to my October birthdate; I'm a real Libra, looking for a way to balance arguments on both sides.

Amsterdam certainly has shaped my opinions, and the richness of all the possibilities constantly broadens your perspective. The city coerces you into thinking about yourself and what you really want to do, who you really want to be. That's because the city gives you those possibilities; it's difficult to avoid them.

I ask Cohen what he is proud of, expecting him to refer to the period after the murder of Theo van Gogh – a turbulent time in Amsterdam's recent history. He smiles in answer and surprises me.

Okay, this is perhaps a cliché, but I am proud of my children. I am not involved with them as much these days, as naturally they go their own way as they get older, but it's so nice to see them change and develop.

If I have to talk about achievements in my work, well, I'm glad that I had the possibility to play a role in the very necessary issue of bringing people together. On the other hand, I'm not proud of that as such, because it is simply part of my identity. It wasn't a choice. My way of doing things, bringing together to resolve differences, comes with my character – that is who I am.

After the murder of Theo van Gogh, there was clearly a lot of frustration and anger, a lot of extremism in the air. It was important to face that, so on the first night after the incident we encouraged the public to come to Dam Square and make a lot of noise, to get their feelings out in the open. This was an important moment.

I felt instinctively that I had to speak there, even though it wasn't easy because some of the anger was directed towards me.

Nevertheless, I thought, *I am the mayor. I must be visible and take responsibility*. I think it was a good speech because on one side I tried to evoke and reflect the angry sentiments, yet on the other side – well, I am a calm person, and this quietness helped to settle the crowds down.

If you don't behave in a way that is true to yourself, others immediately see through the pretence – but if you really act in a way that is a part of you, the public see that and they feel it, and it gains trust.

Outside of Amsterdam there was a lot of trouble with rioting, and that threatened to overflow into our city. Some groups were saying, "You have to beat up the Muslims, it's war!" But I couldn't behave that way – I had to try bringing both sides together. There was no other way for me. So all this noise and shouting to be rough on Muslims didn't make much impression on me. That's not my style.

Cohen is realistic about changes in the level of tolerance in Amsterdam, but is keen to make clear that these are a reflection of general changes in society, rather than just in Amsterdam. As we talk, I begin to realise something remarkable; that he is first and foremost a person, and secondly a politician.

There are definitely more tensions now than in the past among the various cultures in Amsterdam, tensions which are also being felt across Europe. You have to look wider to understand and address your own problems; for example, look at Germany and their difficulties with multiculturalism, how the Roma are being ejected from France, the row in the USA about the mosque near Ground Zero... Tensions between different groups in society are bigger than they used to be.

But coming back to Amsterdam: it is more difficult now for all kinds of minorities, like Jews and homosexuals, to live in the city, you see there is more separation between minority groups than there was back in 2001. Those are trends that have to be stopped; they're simply not in line with the real meaning of this city.

The media have their part to play in this. Often they say it's only Moroccans and Turks causing the problems, but that's not true – it's an exaggeration.

It's always difficult to take a step towards 'different' individuals: *Het vreemde vinden wij vreemd* [We find strange things strange.] It's sadly a very true cliché, and not one I like at all.

My saying *[de boel bij elkaar houden]* is all about tolerance, respect and a kind of openness. We always have to exchange views – it doesn't mean we have to agree, and you can be very clear about those differences – but in doing so, you have to keep a tone of respect and perspective.

The attitude of Amsterdammers towards each other has long been, "You are different from me – so what? Do what you like!" As a lawyer I always add to that, 'within the limits of the law.' If you don't agree with the rules and behave unlawfully or cause a nuisance, then naturally it's difficult for others to behave with tolerance towards you.

There's a knock on the door and, as promised, Ahmed Marcouch appears. Cohen immediately encourages him to be part of the book, in a way that is inclusive, not demanding. He clearly gets a small kick out of bringing these two people together. *[See page 38 for the interview with Marcouch.]*

One of the most enjoyable aspects of Amsterdam is the biking. It brings everyone onto an equal level – it doesn't matter whether you are a businessman or a cleaner, everybody is the same when cycling.

My favourite view in Amsterdam was from my office in the City Hall. It was quite special; you could see the centuries-old Amsterdam houses and look across the River Amstel and at the cosy cafés alongside it. Everybody finds the canals beautiful, but, in a different way, the new buildings in the former harbour around Oosterdokseiland and Westerdokseiland are just as impressive. Those are redevelopments of old industrial areas to create new, thriving districts – they draw architects from around the world to come and learn. The 17th-century houses are beautiful, but the houses built in the past 20 years are also having an impressive effect on the city.

Despite his easy-going nature, Cohen is not at all afraid to tackle difficult issues. We touch on the subject of the Red Light District and how the image of the city is changing for tourists.

Nobody denies that the Red Light District [RLD] is a part of Amsterdam. Many seem to think the area will be closed, but this is not in the plans at all. It has been there for hundreds of years! Even if the city council wanted to close it – and I personally don't believe they do – it would be impossible; it could never happen.

I wanted to bring down the criminal elements that were controlling parts of the area, and we addressed this by purchasing some buildings and closing down a number of windows. We understood that we didn't control the area any more; that it was under the influence of those you don't want to influence your city. By taking back a part, we could regain control. That was our reason and that's still the reason.

There is prostitution; nobody can ignore that fact. It's impossible to drive it out, and let's also bear in mind that Amsterdam is a commercial city – the RLD is important for the its economy. Nevertheless, there should not be such a high level of criminality.

The RLD is an interesting area, not only because of the prostitution factor, but also because of its many residents. It was getting so crowded that it was nearly impossible to live there any more, so we had to balance the needs of the locals with the role the area plays for Amsterdam. The RLD will remain, albeit in a more controlled way. That was my vision, and that still is my vision.

I'm very much in favour of the Redlight Fashion Amsterdam project, which brought all those creative people into the area and is helping to change its image. Mariette Hoitink made it happen *[see her interview on page 44]* and this is typical Amsterdam: Have the idea and realise it within a very short period. That's a great aspect of the attitude of the locals from this city.

At the time Mr. Cohen and I meet, the Netherlands is a country in political transition while a new coalition government is being formed. I get the impression that he is feeling quite nostalgic for the past life in the capital.

The *I amsterdam* campaign has certainly had a positive influence on

I OFTEN SAID TO THE QUEEN THAT I WAS PRESIDENT OF THE REPUBLIC OF AMSTERDAM IN THE KINGDOM OF THE NETHERLANDS. SHE ALWAYS SMILED AT THAT

how the city is seen in other countries. *[Cohen goes over to a chair in the corner of his office and proudly shows a bag with the logo emblazoned across it.]* The message was developed while I was mayor and I believe that, together with the *ILNY* slogan for New York, it's the best in the world. It tells you something about the quality of the city; how it is made up of the people as a collective, yet the spirit is of individuality.

The profile of visitors is changing – less of those beer drinkers, the ones spending all their money in the coffee shops! It's clear that a lot of visitors are going not only to the RLD, but also to the Van Gogh and Rijksmuseum. It's not either/or.

Amsterdam is simply different from any other capital, and from the rest of the Netherlands. I often said to the Queen that I was president of the Republic of Amsterdam in the kingdom of the Netherlands! She always smiled at that.

One of Cohen's most visible tasks was to carry out the royal marriage of the Queen's son, Willem-Alexander to his bride Máxima. Millions were watching on TV – surely he was nervous? He smiles.

I wasn't worried, because the whole event was very well prepared and organised. You have to keep it small and forget the cameras and viewers – for me, this ceremony was just for the two people in front of me; it was important for them. I think I was less nervous than Máxima was!

www.jobcohen.nl

A *waag* was where all goods were weighed and measured on entry for sale in the city. This 15th-century building was also the setting for a scene depicted in a Rembrandt painting that drew Nina Siegal to Amsterdam.

SO MANY CULTURAL AND DIVERSE EVENTS - THERE'S ALWAYS SOMETHING HAPPENING

NINA SIEGAL

AMSTERDAMMER SINCE 2005
AUTHOR AND EDITOR-IN-CHIEF AT 'TIME OUT AMSTERDAM'
FAVOURITE AMSTERDAM LOCATION — DE WAAG, NIEUWMARKT

Amsterdam is jammed full of contrasts. There's an incredible diversity of cultures and nationalities [177 at the last count!] giving rise to an amazing range of cultural activities and events.

If you want an underground exhibition of street art, you'll find it. Love to hear the best in classical music, or have an urge for the grungiest thrash metal band? It's all here. Events like the multicultural Kwakoe festival and Amsterdam Gay Pride are iconic of the breadth of possibilities in Amsterdam.

Nina Siegal came from New York to Amsterdam on the back of a slight obsession with Rembrandt, a painter who's at the very heart and soul of the city's cultural heritage. Nina's focus was on a particular painting from 1632. As well as her quest, she took on the job as editor of *Time Out Amsterdam*, a monthly English-language cultural magazine that tells the latest about the almost overwhelming selection of Amsterdam's stuff-to-do.

That background gives Nina a unique insight into the connection between Amsterdam's history and its current culture. As soon as I discovered her story, I felt I'd found another piece of the jigsaw of this city's essence.

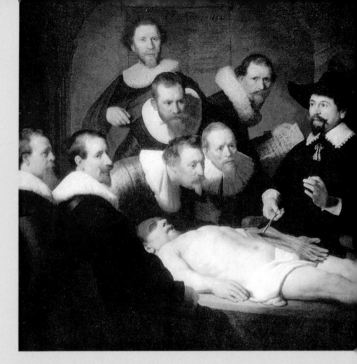

"

A Rembrandt painting brought me to Amsterdam. Honestly!

I was living and studying in Iowa City and my first novel was close to being finished. During my last semester, I took an additional course entitled 'Iconography in Painting', which led to a complete life-change.

Our task was to 'read' a painting and try to find the narrative behind the image. My father was a doctor and he had a copy of Rembrandt's *The Anatomy Lesson of Dr. Nicolaes Tulp* hanging on his wall in his study, as many doctors seem to do. It's one of only a handful of major group portraits by Rembrandt, and depicts eight men in dark cloaks standing around a dead body that's being dissected. That image on my dad's wall had always fascinated me, yet despite being very familiar with it, I had no idea of its story or even who had painted it. So when the professor gave us this assignment, I saw a chance to dig a bit deeper. The story gradually hooked me, until I became a little obsessed with it and it formed the basis of an idea for a new novel.

It was 1632; Rembrandt was 26 years old and had just arrived in Amsterdam from his home town of Leiden. He received a commission to paint a portrait of the Amsterdam Surgeon's Guild, which had commemorative paintings made every five to ten years, as the members of the guild or the head of the guild changed. Lots of artists had been commissioned to paint similar portraits of other groups or guilds, and considered it a good way of paying the bills because each man in the portrait would pay to be included. Many of the resulting pictures from the genre are very static and dull.

Rembrandt was always looking to make a name for himself by going that bit further, so he decided to make his painting more dramatic. He created a scene portraying the doctors gathered around a dead body while a dissection was taking place – something no artist had done before. It was a dynamic scene – rather than just staring out blankly towards the viewer, each person's face is responding to the body, to the doctor and to this extraordinary situation.

We sit outside De Koffie Salon on Cornelis Huygensstraat 82. It's the day of the World Cup final, and vuvuzelas are blaring all around us. The city is orange, as the first of a crowd – which will eventually grow to 180,000 on Museumplein – begin to make their noisy way through the city.

If you go to Nieuwmarkt, you'll see a beautiful 15th-century building in the middle of the square, called De Waag [The Weigh House]. This was the setting of a public dissection that took place on 31 January 1632 and forms the background story to the painting. Over 200 guild members and public came to see that dissection; they literally bought tickets for the 'show', which was considered the highlight of the annual Winter Festival.

It wasn't like today, where an autopsy might be used primarily to teach budding doctors how to do surgery or about the body. Rather, this was used as a forum for a lesson in moral philosophy. It

was about big questions, such as: Where is the soul located in the body? Does any sense of morality reside within the body? And if so, where? That may seem like a funny idea, but we still use expressions like, 'I have a gut feeling' or 'my heart wasn't in it', which take their origin from a belief that emotions have a physical location in the body. This wasn't just an issue for the medical world, but also for society at large, which is why it was a public event. Cutting up a body in public sounds pretty ghoulish to us now, but there was a higher purpose to it at the time.

As I began reading about the painting, I became utterly fascinated. There were so many layers of meaning, the whole thing grabbed me.

At this moment, Nina holds herself back. "I could go on about this..." Yet I feel I've missed something, and sense there is a possible link to Nina's life, that made her choose this painting.

I guess the personal connection is the fact that my Dad is an Aids specialist who was working as chief immunologist at the very beginning of the epidemic. He used to say that he felt like a medieval doctor in that period; just helping people die rather than curing or treating them, because so little was known about how to deal with and treat Aids then. When I was growing up, we were very much in the midst of this 'plague mentality' and I increasingly saw this picture as somehow connected to the Black Death.

What I responded to in the painting is Dr. Tulp. He's standing there very proudly with the strength of his authority, but there's something about how Rembrandt painted the portrait that calls that authority into question. If you look at the faces of the other doctors, you can see doubt and confusion. That feels to me in some way related to my Dad's torment in the very early stages of the

A REMBRANDT PAINTING BROUGHT ME TO AMSTERDAM

epidemic, because he felt unable to deal with the situation with his usual authority, based on knowledge, training and experience.

That's also why I was interested in the true narrative of the story – because I had projected all this stuff onto it already. And that's what brought me to Amsterdam.

I've met lots of people who made a snap decision to come to Amsterdam, based on a wish or whim. I also notice some come as a getaway and for some reason Amsterdam feels like a safe haven. Nina's story seems a combination of all of this, plus a bit of luck.

Once I got the idea for the book, I realised the only way I was going to write it was to move here for a period. I mean, you can't just make stuff up about a place you've never been to! I applied for a Fulbright fellowship to come and research the novel, although I didn't know much about Amsterdam other than having been here for a weekend trip and thinking, *Great place, I could live here.* I guess I was concentrated much more on Rembrandt than the city.

Via a teacher of mine, I got in contact with Ernst van de Wetering, who's considered the number one Rembrandt scholar in the world. He helped me with the research and thanks to him, I came to realise that when you're talking about Rembrandt, you're not really writing about one painter, because everyone has their own version of who he is. The challenge for my book is how to represent a man who has been interpreted in so many different ways, as a character in my novel.

The volume of the crowd in the streets increases – three hours until kick-off. The contrast between the legacy of Rembrandt and the immediacy of the crowd is strong, reflecting the contrasts in Nina's life. While writing her book about the very centre of Amsterdam's

creative and cultural history, she took on the job of editing a magazine about what's happening each month.

My background in journalism supported me to stay and continue my research after my grants had run out. I've been a journalist since 1994, with many different roles – including the urban life and culture reporter for *Bloomberg News* and three years as a reporter for 'The City' section of *The New York Times*. I was doing a little editing and teaching at the now-defunct *Amsterdam Weekly*, and when *Time Out Amsterdam* began, I was asked to be the founding editor.

I knew it would be a huge challenge to launch a magazine from scratch. In fact, it turned out to be an insane task. We started talking around June 2008, and my training in London was in July. Then I had to hire the editorial staff, who started work on September 1st. Our initial issue had to be finished by September 22nd so we could have it ready for our launch party two days later. Three weeks with a brand-new team of writers and designers to create a 100-page magazine? Yes, it was extreme. But sometimes it's best just to set yourself a deadline so you're forced to get up and running.

Amsterdam is a perfect place for *Time Out;* a city bubbling with so many culturally diverse events. It's small but it's dense, has a cosmopolitan feel and yet still keeps that local atmosphere. A constantly changing expat community is a source of new input and there's a pretty good writing community here. The ease of being an English speaker here also influenced my decision to stay. Learning the local language as a foreigner in any city is always an advantage, but there's a big English-speaking culture here – TV, music and comedy. That reduces the boundaries between the expat and local communities, unlike in places like Madrid or Paris, where you must speak the local language to get by at all.

My biggest impression of Amsterdam is its internationalism. Ever since Rembrandt's time, it's been like that, continually looking out to the rest of the world for resources. Being such a small city in a small country meant having to import a lot to be successful. A multicultural nature is essentially the engine of this place – it's always been a crossroads for people coming and going. Understandably, there are Hollanders who don't like so many foreigners being here, but that internationalism here has been the core of so much for at least 400 years.

I know that Nina has been working for quite some years on her book, so I'm almost hesitant to ask how it's going.

Ah, 'the relevant question!' I have a lot written, over 400 pages, and a lot of characters on the page. When others read it, they tell me they love the sections, so I receive a lot of encouragement. The danger is that I can easily get immersed in the research, because the subject is so rich and interesting. However, as one fellow writer told me: at some point you have to box up your research, put it in the attic and write the book as a novelist, not as a historian. I've done that and am on the way to finishing. I hope Rembrandt will **be proud** of me!

www.ninasiegal.com

THERE'S SOMETHING FUNDAMENTALLY AMSTERDAM-LIKE ABOUT THE WAY THE CLUB OPERATES - EVERYTHING IS BASED ON EMOTION

With its rebellious and creative spirit, Amsterdam was perhaps destined to be a platform for pirate radio in the days before the broadcasting industry was opened up. That deregulation happened in the '90s in Holland. Before then, a man like Daniël Dekker had to find creative ways to share his ideas of what current music was really all about.

These days, he's a more familiar figure as part of mainstream radio – he even co-presents the Eurovision Song Contest on Dutch TV. He's also very much involved with his other passion, Ajax football club.

Nevertheless, Daniël still has a keen eye for new music. "You have to look out for these guys," he tells me, mentioning a new Dutch band. "They're going to be big, really big!" Even after three decades in the business, he can still get that buzz from a new musical spirit coming through.

We meet in Café Krull in *de Pijp*, a dynamic area of the city with many alternative bars and cafés, and find we share two passions – music and football.

DANIËL DEKKER

BORN IN AMSTERDAM

OVER 30 YEARS IN BROADCASTING

FAVOURITE AMSTERDAM LOCATION — VONDELPARK

"Normally, your favourite places relate to memories and your history. I know Vondelpark is not loved by everyone, but my memories of it are really strong because I grew up around there. Later, when I got into music, I loved going to the open-air concerts, to see so many bands perform. These days, those events still take place during June and July. In the past, it was not as organised; everyone just sat on the grass, smoked a joint and watched a band like Doe Maar play for three hours. Now they have proper seats, a good stage and excellent sound, and it's still very atmospheric to see a vibrant open-air Vondelpark concert in the sun on a Sunday afternoon.

My other favourite place in the city is around the Kinkerstraat, because that's where I started at the pirate station, Radio Decibel, in the early '80s. That was not a good time for Amsterdam, because there was a serious housing shortage. A lot of areas needed major renovation and the economy wasn't going well at all. It was almost like life was being lived in black and white! So we thought, *Let's do something for people, give them something to be happy about.* Music can do that.

The studio itself was a place where young people met – artists, painters, musicians... It was a creative spot in the heart of the city. The radio station was only open at the weekends, so we would start on Friday at 6 pm and go on until 9 pm on Sunday. For the rest of the week, we did 'normal' jobs – I was working in a bank for many years!

Daniël's next radio station, after Decibel, had a creative method of getting around the outdated broadcasting regulations.

I joined Radio 10 FM, the first commercial station in the Netherlands, which was officially based in Italy. We would record the programmes here, in a studio on PC Hooftstraat, and send them over to some Dutch colleagues living in Milan. They would broadcast – in Dutch – to the Italians and of course nobody there understood or listened to it. The real purpose was to use the [then new] satellite systems to broadcast back into Holland. Bizarrely, according to Dutch law, that was fine! We didn't get an official frequency until 10 years later.

That period was special, because rock music in the '80s seemed to be an important part of everyone's life. Listeners would be waiting in anticipation for weeks to hear the first play of the latest single by their favourite band on the radio station. Well, times change, and dance and house music were very quickly adopted by Amsterdam in the '90s. I began to notice that development when DJ'ing at parties and somebody would come up to ask for *Thunderdome XV, track three.* They didn't ask for the artist or name of the song, but a number. Nevertheless, I still love to work in music because a good song can make you happy, sad, or help you reach for something.

It doesn't take long for Amsterdammers to get onto the subject of Ajax. Daniël is president of their supporters' club, so it's no surprise when he begins talking about the team.

Ajax has been a part of my Amsterdam experience since I was just eight years old, when I went along with my grandfather to watch the games at De Meer. Nowadays that stadium is extremely romanticised; in reality it had aged so much, we simply had to move. For instance, you could smell the stink of the toilets everywhere, but now the older fans reminisce and think that was fantastic – they even say things like, "Oh, I really miss that piss-air."

We had to change stadium to go further as a club, and the new Arena in the south-east of Amsterdam is perhaps still not a real home. Well, listen to me calling it 'new' – when Ajax moved there already in 1996! It takes a long time to settle in, and we need a big success to celebrate there. It's the same when you move into a new house – first you need to have a big party, then it becomes home.

Our team has struggled in recent years, which led us to do some research among all kinds of people associated with the club. The conclusion is clear – everything to do with Ajax is based on feelings and not rationale. It's a major company with a multi-million turnover, but there's something fundamentally 'Amsterdam' about the way the club operates on emotion alone. I like that in a way, but I would also like to win!

My favourite recent football memories are of the big fan-parties during the World Cup and European Championships on Museumplein. The city bent the rules a bit by allowing so many big screens and such a big crowd for the World Cup final in 2010 – 180,000 in one place! – and those gatherings always happen without any trouble. Everyone's in orange and either happy or sad, but all of us together.

Dutch music has not had much exposure outside of Holland, but there is one band that, for Daniël, expresses the essence of Amsterdam.

It has to be De Dijk – partly because I grew up with their special kind of soul and rock 'n' roll, and partly because they're also very 'Amsterdam'; just being themselves, keeping their identity as individuals and as a band. The guys hop on the bike, grab a beer and play together. They recognise that no-one can feel especially privileged due to their social status or what they do for a living in this city. Whether you work for the radio, in a band or behind the bar, you're all equal. And that's the way you're treated, too. Amsterdammers speak quite bluntly, so if they think you're getting above yourself, just because of a bit of success, they'll tell you!"

www.goudenuren.nl
www.ajaxlife.nl

IN AMSTERDAM, BEING DIFFERENT WAS SOMETHING TO BE FLAUNTED AND PROUD OF

PETER VAN DER MEULEN

AMSTERDAMMER SINCE 1986
CREATOR OF 'MEUBEL STUKKEN' EVENTS COMPANY
FAVOURITE AMSTERDAM LOCATION – DE BIJLMER

Meubel Stukken is a company that organises Electronic Dance music parties under brands like Rauw, Oud Hollandsch Acid Feest and Speedfreax. Another major event, called Valtifest, is organised together with MTV. One of the company's creators, Peter van der Meulen, epitomises the contradictions that Meubel Stukken revel in; a calm and slightly shy kind of guy, it's hard to imagine him as one of the pioneers of the acid house music revolution in the '90s.

He has created such a large network of creative and supportive artists that he has just three permanent employees. Peter's company is a reflection of one aspect of Amsterdam's culture. Large numbers work part-time or for more than one company or project in this city. Especially in the creative industry, people are masters of many different skills and apply them for money or for free, depending on the circumstances of whoever is providing the platform. That's the true essence of Amsterdam's entrepreneurship.

I was intrigued by a photo of Peter dressed as a circus ringmaster that hangs on the wall at the office which we share. Could this be the same man I see regularly, quietly sorting through receipts and invoices at his desk?

A friend of mine was asked to become the manager of this new club that was going to be opened, called RoXY, and he asked me to be his assistant manager. I'd lived a pretty quiet life in Haarlem, which is a much smaller city just west of Amsterdam, so when I moved at the age of 27, I was thrown in at the deep end of Amsterdam's nightlife.

I had no idea the RoXY would become an icon of Amsterdam's party culture, but we did start out very big. The day before the official opening, MTV Europe staged their launch party there – unfortunately the club wasn't even finished yet! We had to serve the drinks from the cellar because the bars weren't complete and MTV's American production company drilled holes all over this beautiful building to hang the sound and lighting equipment. Still, it was a big success and the RoXY quickly became one of the busiest clubs in town.

From the moment of the launch, everything was new for me. That was the first place I saw a transvestite, for example – there were none in Haarlem! And though I had known some gay people, nobody was open about it. Yet here it was flaunted as something to be proud of, and I loved the show of it all. Soon this fantastic house music revolution came about and I was absolutely hooked. Originally I'd thought I would stay at the club for a year or two; in the end it lasted ten years for me.

How Peter went on to become an entrepreneur in Amsterdam's party scene is one of those 'it can just happen in this city' stories.

Joost van Bellen was a DJ and the artistic director at the RoXY. We had some ideas about showing everybody how we thought partying should be. It was around the time when speed garage was getting popular, and the economy was going well too – it was becoming more common to drink champagne, eat oysters and dress up in a more stylish way when going out.

The first party we established was called Speedfreax and it took place in the old gasworks, the Westergasfabriek. It's now one of Amsterdam's most popular cultural centres, but at that time nobody staged parties in empty factories. Partygoers preferred to stay in the centre, within the canal circle, but we drew them there with a new concept and environment. It was difficult because we didn't have that much money, but a lot of friends came and helped us or the acts worked for free. We put all our money into building a fabulous décor and charged a lot of money – 35 guilders, which is about 16 euros now. That was the price of one Ecstasy pill in those days!

We created a completely new way of going out by adding some class and style. A dress code of no jeans allowed was strictly set, and you had to make a reservation and show ID at the door. Instead of just music, it was a whole attitude and experience.

This was a success and we carried on creating new party concepts. To begin with, it was all very unofficial, and only later did we form our company, Meubel Stukken. Translated into English, it means 'furniture', but 'Meubel' is a combination of Joost's and my second names. We liked it because it didn't sound typically 'let's party!' Often our ideas are based on contradictions.

Everything just happened to me. I like to go with the flow and you could say I never really made any serious decisions in my life. I studied initially as a computer programmer, made a big change to being a stylist, and finally ended up by accident in club management. The only time I really made a proper decision was in forming Meubel Stukken. Joost was the creative guy musically and I had ideas as an entrepreneur – that combination worked really well.

After another 10 years, we started creating festivals, one of which is Valtifest, held at the end of the summer festival season. Last year it took place in Amsterdam Noord at the former NDSM shipyard – perfect for a loud, outdoor party.

Peter is originally from Rotterdam and he's very relaxed about the standard friction between that city's people and those of the capital.

Having being born in Rotterdam means I'm a Feyenoord football club supporter. The pity is that Rotterdammers tend to have this inferiority complex towards the capital. We've presented some events there, and always somebody comes onto the microphone saying, "Hey Amsterdam, see what we've got!"

If you live in a place for a long time, you become from that place and I do think of myself as an Amsterdammer. I love the Bickerseiland, just west of the central station. This area has real history and you can still see where the small boats were made in workshops around the canals there. I also like the Begijnhof on Spui for a similar reason. It's a small back-street garden surrounded by houses from the 14th century and if you go there on a quiet day, it's almost like being in a time machine, taking you back centuries.

I live in Amsterdam Zuidoost [south-east] now. Earlier I lived on the Egelantiersgracht, which I believe is the most beautiful canal in Amsterdam, but a friend recommended living in Zuidoost because it's so green and spacious. In some ways I was typically Amsterdam; even though Zuidoost is only a few kilometres away, I'd never been there. Amsterdammers tend to stick to their own boundaries and think of anything outside of the city centre as farmyards!

There's that picture of Peter in the office, dressed up as a circus ringmaster. It's completely different to the man I know, who is far more understated.

That's from a party we did with photographer Erwin Olaf, which had a circus theme. We always give our parties a dress theme, because then the audience can become somebody different to their daily self and behave in a more extrovert way. That gives me the chance to be something different too.

www.meubelstukken.nl

Sometimes it's easy to see where a picture has been taken in Amsterdam, but Pim Kops revels in keeping his audience guessing about the facts of his city photography.

MY AMSTERDAM PHOTOGRAPHY IS NOT ABOUT THE FACTS, IT'S ABOUT A WAY OF SEEING THE CITY

PIM KOPS

AMSTERDAMMER SINCE 1963

KEYBOARD PLAYER OF 'DE DIJK', PHOTOGRAPHER AND ARTIST

FAVOURITE AMSTERDAM LOCATION — SPIEGELSTRAAT

At the very beginning of my search for the essence of Amsterdam, film-maker Suzanne Raes *[see her interview on page 122]* guided me to Pim Kops. Sure enough, her assertion that his photography was capturing that essence turned out to be true.

As the keyboard player in Amsterdam band De Dijk, Pim has gigged across the Netherlands for 30 years. Despite their national popularity, there is something intrinsically 'Amsterdam' about the group. They've written countless songs about different aspects of the Amsterdam experience, and seem able to capture what it's like to sit in a Jordaan bar on a Saturday evening with friends, low light and beer.

Pim's creativity extends way beyond music, though. He's a self-taught artist in drawing and painting, and his photographs are a testament to his strong connection to his home city. Over a nine-month period, I came to understand the elements of a true 'Pim pic' and to see Amsterdam in a different way. He's taken hundreds of great photographs, both in colour and in black and white, many of which are showcased on his Facebook site.

Listening to him describe how he developed his approach helped me understand how creative individuals in this city are able to apply themselves to a variety of artistic pursuits. His co-operation in providing so many photographs for this book is in tune with the general sense of support I've felt from the people who shape the essence of Amsterdam.

It's hard to say what a true Amsterdammer is. My ancestors have lived here for centuries and although I wasn't born here, I went to school in Amsterdam, and my parents and grandparents lived here. In reality, every Amsterdammer has roots elsewhere; until the 12th century, this region was just a swamp, while other cities were already developing. Amsterdam would not exist without people coming from other areas. Johan van der Keuken, a documentary film-maker, came up with the description 'global village', accurately capturing the idea that this is one of the greatest melting pots of the world.

Pim assures me that he has never studied history. However, his father, who is an art historian and worked at the Rijksmuseum for many years, clearly inspired a passion for his home city's historical roots.

Historically Amsterdam has been a crossroads for all kinds of cultures and crafts. It was famous for map-making, and was the home of numerous book printers at a time when it was illegal in many countries to print certain political or religious content. Amsterdam's authorities saw this as business and tolerated it, in the same way that various religions were given the space to express themselves. You can see a good example of this in the Koepelkerk, the large domed Lutheran church on Singel. The Lutherans and other religions were not allowed to build high spires, so they built a dome that was very wide instead, which you could think of as a practical joke. When locals and sailors looked in from the harbour in centuries past, they would see this symbol of a non-state faith well before they saw the Protestant Westerkerk.

Amsterdam's longest standing band took their name from something integral to the city, despite their influences coming from a variety of different sources.

When Amsterdammers go shopping, they might say, "I'm just going to the *dijk*." In fact there are a number – such as Haarlemmerdijk, Nieuwendijk, and Zeedijk – but your friends will know you mean the nearest of those to your house. Dykes are the mounds of earth that were originally built to prevent the water from flooding the Netherlands, so the name of our band is very much part of the city, and indeed of the whole country.

My musical heroes when I was growing up were artists like Bob Dylan, Neil Young and The Beatles, as well as Bach and Ravel. From the beginning, De Dijk's music has contained influences from rhythm and blues, as well as soul, so it was pretty logical to make an album with legend Solomon Burke in 2010. He was one of the pioneers of soul music in the '60s – such a shame he passed away last year.

Favourite location to perform? It has to be Paradiso – that's the place. Being a typical Amsterdam church with wooden balconies gives it an amazing shape and atmosphere. Part of the magic for the audience as well as the performers is the history of all the huge bands that have

played there – the Stones, Nirvana, even the Sex Pistols. That makes the place feel bigger than reality. De Dijk is also part of Paradiso's history, as we play there at least three days in a row every year. I must have been on that stage over a hundred times! But it's still special every time.

Over the past months, I've met Pim on many occasions to talk about pictures for the book. We've discussed music, yet he's at his most animated when sharing his passion for photography.

When I was in high school, I learned about developing film in the darkroom. That was the old-fashioned way of picking up photography and it still helps when I process digital images. Certain concepts of finalising pictures remain the same, regardless of whether you do it by hand or computer. For some years I was distracted by my video camera. I returned to still photography when mobile phones began to include cameras, about 10 years ago, because I always carried my phone with me. Naturally the quality was not very high, but my interest in still pictures was sparked again and I bought a very good Leica compact camera.

Four major themes interest me. I've taken thousands of pictures of De Dijk from my unique position at the back of the stage. This is different to most concert photographs, which are usually from the audience's point of view: I show the venue, as well as the band and audience, from my point of view. My camera is great because you just press the button and the camera will only take a picture once it has found its focus. *[I've seen Pim doing this – playing keyboards with one hand and setting his camera with the other.]*

Amsterdam is my second theme. I simply love taking photographs of this city; it's the most amazing set any director could wish for, thanks to the architecture, the canals and special light. The city is at the core of the two other themes – black and white, and colour. I also have photographs of other settings in these two categories, like *Het Gein*, a little river close to Amsterdam. Still, the majority of my pictures are taken in my city.

I often go exploring after a gig, spending one or two hours just looking for good images and scenes. I lose myself in my photography during the night and get into a kind of trance. It's maybe 3 am, I'm completely alone and I take my bike through the streets and canals. It's a sort of adventure, almost a quest, and I'm aware of all those special elements that make a classic picture: light, dark, grey, composition, balance, and sometimes movement. These come together in a partly unconscious way; I know those elements are working in the background when I am taking photos.

Look at the picture of the Wilhelmina statue on Rokin as an example [see page 10]. I was biking around the area and happened to notice two very bright lamps that were quite ugly. It came to me that if I positioned the camera in a certain way, the light could become a part of the scene and help me create those elements of light and dark contrast, give a certain tone to the picture. I waited a long time to capture the particular moment – in fact, I took many shots – and it was when the cab drove past that the element of movement entered. It completed the shot.

The way I approach photography can be compared to the way I

make music. There are the technical skills – such as knowing how to play the instrument – and there is the extra level of inspiration and interaction with the environment, especially when you're onstage. In my photography, it's the same. I have the knowledge of composition and how to manage and play with the light and tone, which I use in my drawing and painting too. All of these skills are there, but not always in a conscious way. In the end, the photograph is about capturing and expressing a feeling, and allowing the viewers to have their own feeling about the image.

My photography is not about the facts, like the exact location, objects appearing in the shot or timing. It's about a way of *seeing* these things. I often return to the same places, because the light and weather are never the same and the many possible variations in cropping are a never ending adventure.

A long line of artists have captured the Amsterdam and Dutch landscapes on both canvas and film, and Pim sees himself firmly as a part of that line.

I feel there is something going on in the development of my photography that refers back to painters of the past. The way we look at the Dutch landscape today is influenced by the great Dutch artists who painted or drew it throughout the centuries. When we see a small river with a windmill and a cart, subconsciously we feel the paint through it. All those inputs of art, built up over many years, colour our way of seeing.

While walking through Amsterdam streets and canals, I feel as if the work of photographers like Bernard Eilers, George Breitner and Jacob Olie is surrounding me. I've seen a lot a lot of their photography, as well as great art from the past, and it all constantly has an influence. It's almost an addiction to look for a location, find the right moment, an intriguing composition and balance of light. The photographs in this book are the outcome of my way of looking, and I have hundreds more – I'm taking new pictures almost every day.

www.facebook.com/pimkopspage, www.dedijk.nl

I DIDN'T HAVE TO GO AFTER MADONNA – SHE CAME TO AMSTERDAM

A typical Amsterdam approach of keeping things in perspective has helped Egbert create an amazing career as a director to the world's music stars. His diverse credits include broadcasting concerts by Prince and Madonna live to millions on TV, as well as six years directing Sesame Street. Yet he keeps a profile as low as the Netherlands itself; you won't find a single picture of him on the Internet.

EGBERT VAN HEES

AMSTERDAMMER SINCE 1951
TV CONCERT DIRECTOR/BROADCASTER
FAVOURITE AMSTERDAM LOCATION – HIS BOAT ON THE CANALS

As in many cities, there was a turning point in Amsterdam around the '60s. The city was already a very nice place, but the mentality changed during the 'flower power' period. People started to love each other, to trust and respect each other. The Beatles told us to think in a certain way and because they were heroes, we followed them. John Lennon was here at the Hilton for a week, in a big white bed with Yoko Ono, and they preached only peace and love. That era was maybe the seed of a special feeling in Amsterdam and it stayed here much more than in many other cities.

Do you know that Jack Nicholson has an apartment here? Madonna too, and many other stars – they like it because they can walk down the street without getting mobbed. Amsterdam is a healthy place for a successful person to live. I've seen friends who moved to Los Angeles or New York get themselves into trouble, because they lost themselves in the hype of the TV and movie business. Amsterdammers' attitudes keep you very grounded.

The city definitely influenced me in the way I handled some of my projects. When I directed Madonna, live from Rome, there were 150 million watching, so I was under pressure to make it perfect. It's a big risk taking on a task that size, because if you fail, she fails – and then you're finished. But during that show I just focused on my own life and my own work, kept it all in perspective like a typical Amsterdammer. *If she performs badly, there's nothing I can do about it.* The same if the stadium falls down! I concentrate on myself and what I think is best at that moment.

I took that attitude with all of the big shows I directed – Prince, Tina Turner, Lionel Richie. And that seems to work with these stars; I never had to advertise. My breakthrough came with Lionel, because his manager was also Madonna's. I didn't have to come after her – she came to Amsterdam to get me!

Perhaps my favourite Amsterdam music experience was when Michael Jackson came to the city in 1977. He was very young and still in The Jackson 5 then, and his management wanted advice on all kinds of aspects of the show. There was a dance floor in front of the stage, and although there were lots of kids around, they were all too scared to dance. Then my son, who was just 14 at the time, went into the middle of the floor with his girlfriend and danced for Michael Jackson!

Visitors expect Amsterdam to be filled with millions of people. When they learn just how small the city really is, it's always something of a shock. I remember when the filmstar Danny Kaye came to Amsterdam; he was amazed at how small the city was compared to Los Angeles. He wanted a real Dutch restaurant, and I told him, "The best one I know is in Bussum, but that's a rather long way away." He asked how far and I told him, "At least 25 minutes by car." He just laughed and said, "If you drive 25 minutes in LA, you're still in LA!"

www.veronicastory.nl/egbert-van-hees

THE MAKERS OF AMSTERDAM...
THE ESSENCE

Creating a colour book featuring twenty five diverse Amsterdammers was never going to be possible alone. By creative co-incidence, I met these three Amsterdam professionals who added their own unique skills to the book. Joost is a former colleague of mine from Canon: his portrait photography has injected a deeper dimension of visual insight into the character of Amsterdam's essence. Sarah happened to be working in the same shared office space that I took a desk in: her speed of thought and quality in design are incomparable. Anique is not only a PR genius: she's also a contact-maker extraordinaire, combined with the ultimate can-do attitude.

Amsterdam is a small city that anyone can cross easily by bike, always with the possibility of running into familiar faces at any moment. Yet it's one of the most influential cities of the world, in touch with the latest trends and developments in fashion, design and art.

For me, this diversity of cultures and free minds in such a small area forms a breeding ground for innovation and creativity. As a photographer I am happy that I am shaped by this city.

JOOST VAN MANEN
Joost van Manen Photography
www.joostvanmanen.com

Amsterdam has a certain magic about it, you see and feel it everywhere - from the stunning architecture, to the unique people and mix of cultures. I love the vibe in this city: it's a pleasure to live and work here.

SARAH LOUGHRAN
Graphic & Web Designer, Sphere Design
www.spheredesign.biz

Amsterdam, the Metropole of freedom: allowing me to be who I want to be, it respecting me for what I am striving for and embracing me with its most beautiful surroundings. Amsterdam, the city where I and my business were born, raised, and will continue to grow. Amsterdam, the city I love.

ANIQUE VAN DER HULST
Founder, Nineteen PR
www.nineteen.eu

HET LAATSTE WOORD - YOUP VAN 'T HEK

Amsterdam. De stad die je haat en liefhebt tegelijk. Je woont er omdat je er moet wonen. Je kunt niet anders.

Er is van alles mis: de musea zijn veel te lang dicht wegens verbouwing, de halve stad verzakt door de aanleg van een onzinnig metrolijntje, de voetbalclub Ajax is al jaren geen kampioen meer, de grachten zijn in de zomer een soort kermisattractie met dronken provincialen die lallen, hard lallen, keihard lallen, enzovoort, enzovoort...

Zoveel redenen om te verhuizen... en toch kom je er niet weg. Waarom niet? Omdat de stad mooi is, leuk is, gezellig is, goed is... de kroegen zijn bruin, diep donkerbruin, de terrassen gezellig, de nachten zijn er zacht en de theaters bulderen hier net een graadje harder dan elders. De prettige geur van weed, de stoned uit hun ogen kijkende toeristen die zo aandoenlijk knullig fietsen, de glijdende rondvaartboten...

Amsterdam: mijn in de Jordaan geboren vader kon er op schelden, net als zijn broers en zussen, tantes en ooms in wier periferie ik ben opgegroeid... Amsterdamser kon het bijna niet... en ik scheld er ook op, net als mijn kinderen het weer doen, die schelden omdat we zo houden van die stad waar het altijd file is en waarvan de helft van de straten open ligt en... die heerlijke stad met zijn geurende markten, zijn duizend kleuren mensen, zijn rafelranden, zijn rare winkels, zijn leuke, lekkere restaurantjes, die stad die ik zo vaak fluister. Amsterdam!

Amsterdam. The city you hate and love at the same time. You live there because you have to live there. There is no other option.

Lots of things are wrong: the museums are closed for far too long due to renovation, half the city is sinking into the ground because of the construction of a ridiculous metro line, the football club Ajax hasn't been champion in years, the canals in summer are a kind of carnival attraction with drunken provincials who jabber, loudly jabber, deafeningly jabber, etcetera, etcetera...

So many reasons to move away... and still you can't leave. Why not? Because the city is beautiful, is fun, is intimate, is good... the cafés are brown, a deep dark brown, the terraces are welcoming, the nights are balmy and the roar in the theatres is just a tad more boisterous than elsewhere. The sweet aroma of weed, the stoned look in the eyes of tourists whose clumsy bicycle-riding is so touching, the gliding canal boats...

Amsterdam: my father, born in the Jordaan district, could rail at it, just like his brothers and sisters, aunts and uncles in whose circle I was brought up... it didn't get more Amsterdam than that... and I do too, I rail at it as my children do in their turn, rail because we love this city so much, a place where the traffic's always bad and half the streets have been torn up and... that delightful city with its markets full of scents, its people in a thousand colours, its ragged edges, its strange shops, its pleasant, tempting little restaurants, the city I whisper so often. Amsterdam!

Translation: Marinca Kaldeway

PHOTOGRAPHY

Joost van Manen

Inside cover, 5, 9, 13, 14, 15, 17, 21, 22 (2), 29, 30 (TR), 33, 39, 40, 41, 45, 47, 61, 75, 76 (2), 77, 78, 83, 84, 86 (B), 91, 92, 93, 94 (9), 105, 106, 107, 111, 112, 117, 118, 119 (2), 127, 129, 131, 135, 136 (TL), 149 (3)

Pim Kops

2, 10, 18, 26, 34, 42, 50, 58, 64, 72, 80, 88, 96, 102, 108, 114, 124, 132, 142, 145, 146 (2), 147

Katherine Matthews - 6, 7, 8

© Copyright ANP-MMP – 23

Jan Versweyveld – 25 (Halina Reijn in *La voix humaine* - Toneelgroep Amsterdam)

Julia Willard – 36

Caro Bonink 37

Book; *Mijn Hollandse Droom* by Ahmed Marcouch; Publisher, *Contact* - 38

Mylou Oord – 44 (G+N), 48 (Jan Taminiau), 49 (And Beyond) [Redlight Fashion Amsterdam]

Petrovsky & Ramone – 46 (T - And Beyond), (BR - Marije de Haan - winner Lichting 2010), (BL - Floor Kolen) [DUTCH FASHION HERE & NOW@Shanghai Fashion Week]

Fenske Everhartz – 53, 56 (2) (T - *The Essence of Amsterdam*, B - *Aan de Amsterdamse*, both painted by Pascal Griffioen)

Emel Omer – 62

Marc Deurloo – 67, 68 (BL), 71

Dennis Duijnhouwer – 68 (T)

Dennis Bouman – 69 (T), 70 (2), 140

Jan Kees Helms – 85 (copyright, Mariska Majoor)

Iwona Grabowska – 98

Arjen Veldt – 99, 100

Brianna Scott – 101

Blair Prentice – 113

Marcel Ozymantra – 120 (*The Architects Decision*) 121 (*Shock of Daylight*), both painted by Marcel Ozymantra

Frenk van der Sterre - 122

Hristina Tasheva – 123 (T), (B – still from film De Huizen van Hristina, directed by Suzanne Raes)

Guillaume Ehrenfeldt – 128

The Anatomy Lesson of Dr. Nicolaes Tulp, by Rembrandt van Rijn; reproduced courtesy of Royal Cabinet of Paintings, Mauritshuis, The Hague - 136

Björn Martens – 138

Hans Peter van Velthoven – 139

Edwin von Warmerdam - 141

Bob Bronshoff - 150

T=Top, R=Right, L=Left, B=Bottom

A number in brackets indicates more than one image from the photographer on that page.

Every attempt has been made to contact all photographers. If you believe there has been a breach of copyright, please contact the publisher;

DJB Pubs, Tussen de Bogen 24, 1013, Amsterdam

COMING SOON FROM DAVID BECKETT

The Essence™ is a new series of books, which tell the story of a city in the words of the people who shape it. The first features Amsterdam: other major world cities will follow. The question is, which should be the next - London? Shanghai? Buenos Aires? San Francisco? Sydney?

Find out more about further titles in the series at *www.theessenceonline.com*

For exclusive videos and additional content, go to *www.youtube.com/user/theessenceonline*

BUSINESS TITLES

The Three-Minute Presentation

Public speaking can often be a nerve-wracking task: doing it under time-pressure might seem even harder. Yet if you can manage to communicate your message in three minutes, you're able to give any kind of presentation to every type of audience.

Beckett has made hundreds of presentations to thousands of people around the world, and built his business reputation on outstanding communication skills and leadership.

In this new publication, he shares valuable exercises and methods to help you gain all the confidence and skill you need to convince in just three minutes.

A supporting workshop will also be available.

49 tips for the New Entrepreneur

Beckett spent twenty successful years in Sales and Marketing roles with photography company Canon, before taking on the challenge of becoming an entrepreneur. He went on to create The Essence™ brand and establish his own publishing company.

In this new title, David shares his experiences of making the journey from the stability and structure of the corporate world to the open seas of entrepreneurship.

Practical examples, resources and tools will help you to make that transition and prepare you for the tests ahead, as you move towards making your own business dreams come true.

A supporting workshop will also be available.